HAROLD DE   .D

WELCOME
home

Essays and Reflections
from Confinement
to Community

WELCOME

Essays and Reflections
from Confinement
to Community

HAROLD DEAN TRULEAR, PH.D.

Introduction

On Monday, April 4, 2011, I sat on my bunk in the Work Release/Reentry Unit at the George W. Hill Correctional Facility in Delaware County, Pennsylvania. It was just after 4:00 PM, after the afternoon shift change and head count. I knew that in less than two hours, they would call my name, usher me to Property, give me my belongings, and send me out the gate with bus fare. I knew—or at least, hoped—that my godson would be waiting in the parking lot. So, thanks for the bus token, George W. Hill, but I probably won't need it.

They called my name, well, not exactly. The sergeant came on the unit public address system and yelled, "Anybody scheduled to be released today?" I thought that was odd. Shouldn't they know that? I walked slowly to the window and hesitatingly raised my hand in the sergeant's direction. He motioned for a CO to open the door for me.

"YOU!" the CO screamed. "What are you doing here?"

I had been on this unit before and had been transferred back for release the previous Friday. This was his first time seeing me in months, but he remembered me: the guy who asked questions. He had decided months ago that the way to shut me up was to just yell. He hadn't forgotten.

"Just shut up and let us do our job!" he bellowed after the sergeant said he couldn't find my file.

I hadn't said a word. I guess it was just a preemptive strike from a man I had filed away as a blue-collar county resident who couldn't get a job and enjoyed being paid to bully people. I just turned away and went back to my bunk and fought back the tears. As was common on my unit, the correct posture for crying was to face the wall and pretend no one knew you were upset. The man on the bunk across from me knew better.

"Doc," he said, "You all right?"

"They can't find my file, John."

"Hey, man, let me read this to you."

He read Philippians 4 to me. He had no idea that part of the Bible had been my solace reading for the past year I was in "care, custody and control." Whether in a cell, barracks, work release, or house arrest, I had been inmate #10002648 for the past year, and today that was supposed to be over. My eyes were full, but my ears were open.

"The peace of God which passeth all human understanding shall keep your heart and mind. . . . I can do all things through Christ who strengtheneth me. . . . My God shall supply all your needs according to His riches in glory."

I heard John read words that had encouraged me from before the start of my sentence throughout its endurance. I do not know how long it was before I also heard, "Trulear, get in here!" They found my file.

My godson was outside. My family was waiting on me. My church had been praying and writing. I had a relatively good transition home. But I also realized that I was blessed beyond measure to have such support.

Having worked in prisoner reentry before becoming one myself, I could recognize that I had the two most important things a man or woman needs when they are released: a pro-social attitude reflecting a change in my life's direction and pro-social supports, consisting of family, friends, and church members who reinforced the decisions I had made to live life in a manner different than the one that landed me in county jail.

I have spent most of the decade since working and praying to find ways to support those coming out behind me, serving as national director of Healing Communities USA (HCUSA) and teaching courses on the church and criminal justice at Howard University School of Divinity. This devotional is another effort in that work.

Each of the 52 chapters offers a theme for reading and reflection for a week's time. Some are seasonal, such as the ones for New Year's, Easter, Mother's and Father's Day, and Thanksgiving. Others contain general themes that we face on return (and on the way to return) from prison or jail to society. I have written them for as general an audience as I could. Though I am a Christian—and my views reflect this—like the Twelve Step movement, I have tried to keep the focus on spirituality and not religion, principles and not doctrine.

Each chapter also contains seven questions for reflection. I invite the reader to read each chapter for seven days during the week and then answer one question for that week's reading. Spending time with that question, even journaling one's response, can help with the thought processes during reentry. Additionally, the book, with its chapters and reflection questions, can be used in reentry support groups or within a family-and-friends setting in order to draw upon that pro-social support network essential to successful reentry.

If you don't have such support, I suggest you contact a local church, masjid, or house of worship. Contact us at HCUSA (www.healingcommunitiesusa.com), and we can help. This book is part of the HCUSA effort to mobilize congregations to be of such support to individuals and families impacted by incarceration.

My congregation at the time of my release, Praise and Glory Tabernacle of Philadelphia, supported me from arrest, through sentencing and incarceration, all the way to reentry. My current congregation, Shiloh Baptist Church of Alexandria, Virginia, supported the completion of this book. Thank you, Pastors

Phillip Whiteside and Taft Q. Heatley, for being a covering when you could have run for cover.

Special thanks to Rev. Dr. Barbara "Bobi" Wallace for her work in crafting the reflection questions for each chapter. Her insight as a minister and a counselor shines in the provocative questions. They take us out of our comfort zone, which is good because my comfort zone got me locked up in the first place.

Thanks to my nephew Ryan Smith, who helped with the initial editorial work. And thank you, Creator, for the HCUSA movement. All proceeds for this book will go directly to supporting the ongoing work of HCUSA.

Grace and Peace,
Doc

Old Year Out, New Year In (New Year's Day)

New year coming, holding new opportunities. A lot of people will make New Year's resolutions, promises for change. A lot of us made resolutions when we got out, promising to change as well.

"When I get out," said one guy on my block, "I'm not going back to my baby mama. Too much drama."

Another brother said he was through with drugs. Another said he was going to start going to church. I'm sure you made promises to yourself when you got out that things would be different (and I'm not including my man who said when he got out, he was going to jack up his brother-in-law for being a snitch. That's not changing).

Two problems. First, a promise to change can never be fulfilled by a "not" or an "ain't gonna . . ."

You can't "not" do something. You have to say what you're gonna to do instead, because as long as you're focused on the "not," it's still at the front of your mind, pushing you to go back to what got you in trouble in the first place. It's like saying, "Don't think of a fire truck." Well, what did you just do? You thought of a fire truck. "Don't think of a gun." Now the gun is on your mind.

You have to replace thoughts, not just drop them. Replace the gun with "How can I be a peacemaker?" Replace the drugs with "How can I productively ease the tension?" Replace the baby mama drama with "How can I be a good father or mother, despite her or him?" It's not just what you give up; it's what you take on.

Second, a promise doesn't need to wait for an occasion like a new year. Why wait until January 1 to do something you can do today? Why wait until you get home from a bid to try to change your thinking, attitudes, and actions? Sometimes the wait gives you an excuse to continue with foolishness a few more days, which is often just an excuse, and that can mean more problems.

You're gonna stop getting high next year, but that gives you a few days not only to get high, but to get busted on possession. You're gonna stop dealing in the new year, but that holding cell will have a few people there December 31 who just wanted one more day. You're gonna leave him or her in the new year, but I just want some goodbye stuff, and then Jamal or Janelle says hello on September 1. Change it up now while you have a shot at real change without worrying about consequences that can hang over your head.

So it's really not Happy New Year; it's Happy New Day *today*. And if you've already messed up today before you read this, start over. You're allowed. Happy New Minute!

Questions for Reflection:
1. What does it mean to you that your desire to change must be greater than your desire to stay the same?

2. What do you need to do differently to have a more positive desired outcome in your life today?

3. What does the author's statement mean to you when he says, "A promise to change can never be fulfilled by a 'not,' or an 'ain't gonna'?" If you are determined or committed to change, how should you phrase your affirmation? Write it down 25 times in your journal each day.

4. What is the author saying to you when he asserts, "A promise doesn't need to wait for an occasion like a new year?" Why is it important to be determined and in a delayed frame of mind?

5. Why is the phrase "Tomorrow is not promised to us" such an unspoken central point or constant in this devotional?

6. What can you do to change your level of procrastination so that you can make it a Happy New Day every day for the rest of your life?

7. How will you start making each day a "Happy New Day" for the rest of your life? In other words, what positives will you start doing that you have never done before?

Putting Community in Your Corrections

We used to have probation and parole. Now they are called "community corrections," along with any other type of sanctions or punishment that doesn't happen in a prison or jail (like many, I still just say "on paper"). Yes, we are moving into the era of community corrections, where probation, parole, house arrest, diversion programs, and halfway houses all have a new clean name that no one can agree what it means.

For starters, your PO may now be your CSO, community supervision officer. It sounds as if they are serving the community. Maybe yes; maybe no. In some places, it's the same old same old, with a new title. There is a real effort to integrate things such as probation and parole into real communities in other places. For example, in New York City, community supervision offices are actually in real communities, such as Harlem, South Bronx, and Brooklyn, where people live, and community leaders are asked to work with parole officers—I mean, community supervision officers—to help facilitate successful reentry.

In Georgia, CSOs are required to be in the neighborhoods and interact with families to be more supportive of reintegration into society and ditch the "trail 'em, nail 'em, and jail 'em" attitude that too many POs have brandished over the years. That's the kind of attitude that locks up people for what is called a "technical violation," not a new offense, but a failure to comply with probation or parole terms such as paying fines or finding a job. (I guess those two are related!) Failure to appear for an appointment is a technical violation that sometimes occurs because you have to take off from work, which can get you fired, then see "paying fines" above.

Three things are true. First, the system remains punitive before, during, and after incarceration. You have to get a job, and those are hard to find without a criminal record. Tying freedom to finances is similarly punitive. *The New York Times* recently published a study of diversion programs that revealed the difficulty of poor people to pay the fines and costs associated with staying out of jail and the prosecutorial discretion as to who gets into a program and who goes to jail for the same offense. Those who qualify for the programs are part of community supervision. They are often supervised more tightly, resulting in higher levels of revocations. We have to work to change the system.

Second, probation/parole/community supervision officers are like a box of doughnuts: All shapes and sizes in a cramped space. Despite their working conditions, many genuinely care about their clients. Others don't care, and still others "trail 'em, nail 'em"—you know the rest. I've had POs call me "Mister"; I've had POs cuss me out. Most have minimal training compared with the goals initially set for the office, which concerned helping people make the transition home, not serve as mini-police to rack up violations. If community supervision is going to be effective, it will be measured by success stories of those in transition, not in how many people get caught.

Third, those of us who may still be on paper (I had 113 days left on paper when I first wrote this) have a responsibility as well. I may not have liked the way I was held accountable five and a half years after getting out, but part of that is I don't like accountability in any form. I'm a GDI (Google it), and nobody tells me what to do. One thing they tell me to do when I talk like that is to grow up because accountability is part of being an adult, whether it's accountability to my job, my community, or my family.

When *The New York Times* article talked about one case where a mother of five faced revocation of her diversion program because she couldn't afford it, I wondered where was the father—or fathers—of five? IJS. She raised your kids, but you don't have a responsibility to their mother?

There is no community in community corrections. It's just parole and probation, diversion and house arrest with a smooth name. And I've had enough of rough stuff with smooth packages. We need real personal and community participation in community corrections because *community* is not a title; it's where we live. And we need all hands to be accountable, from arbitrary prosecutors and legislatures to cramped line officers, for how people are given second chances. We need change, and we are all accountable.

Questions for Reflections:

1. The author speaks about accountability. Why is accountability necessary?

2. Is accountability necessary in your life? Why or why not? Expound in detail on your answer.

3. As a man or a woman who is a reentering citizen, what responsibilities do you own in being accountable to yourself, your family, and your community?

4. What is meant by "there is no community in community corrections. It's just parole and probation, diversion and house arrest with a smooth name"?

5. How can you be part of a real personal and community participation corrections program?

6. Remember, for something to succeed, we all have a part to play. How can you help jump-start community involvement within your community corrections facilities?

7. Do you know what part you desire in the reorganization process? If so, write it down. If not, take time to research the various positions available to know what role you would like to play in the change.

Welcome Home 3

Minding Your Own Business

Some people think about starting their own business when they come home. There are steps you can take to get ready even before you finish a bid. Or if you are home now, it's not too late to get busy. What should you be doing?

First, check your attitude. Be sure you are committed to making a new start in life. Don't try it; just do it. Your old thinking is what got you the bid in the first place! I remember sitting on the block listening to guys talk about how to beat the system. Yo, if you know how to beat it, what are you doing here? Just stop with the hustle mindset, and determine that you are going to begin fresh.

One crucial component of new thinking is "thinking it through." That means that when something happens, and you are about to react to it, think about the consequences of your actions from beginning to end before you act. You should come up with a different decision than the kind that got you the bid in the first place.

Second, get a positive support group. I know you have been trained to be loyal to a certain crew, but if they won't support you in the changes you want to make, then lose them. People who come home and stay home report that they had a support system that kept their thinking straight. People who want you to go back to old thinking will convince you to revert to old behavior before you can will them over to new thinking. Surround yourself with people who will share your new vision.

Family and friends like that can help you start the business before you get home. They can contact a multilevel marketing company (there are over 50 listed in Google) and get started selling things from home products (Amway) to travel (YTB International) to energy/telecommunications (ACN Inc.) to jewelry (Traci Lynn). They can start selling for you and build a customer base ready for you to build on when you get home. If you think about it, many of us were locked up for multilevel marketing in the first place.

If sales is not your thing, there are other businesses open to you. *Thinking Outside the Blox: a Step-by-Step Guide Teaching Felons and Those Who Risk Becoming Felons 22 Realistic Income-Producing Options* is a great book that has several ideas for business development from exterminators (of pests, that is) to asbestos removal to crime scene cleanup. Michael Brewer, the author, pushes the notion we mentioned earlier: You have to think differently, in this case, outside the blocks. New attitude, new support, new business, new freedom. You have this option!

Questions for Reflections:
1. It should be important to you to stay away from controversial old haunts and former friends. Write down why it is vital for you to change your way of thinking.

2. What is the difference between trying to do something and being determined to do something? And why is it important to understand the difference?

3. Why should you stop and think before you act, react, or speak?

4. What are some criteria you can use in creating a positive support group? Why is it important to surround yourself with positive people who know who they are and their goals in life?

5. Who are the first people you should consult for guidance in the type of home and working environment you need to create for yourself?

6. It is essential to get quiet, think about what you like to do, and find opportunities for schooling or learning that will help you achieve your goals. In so doing, it gives you time to develop realistic goals. Why is this important?

7. Are you ready to research the internet to get started looking for various career paths? Make sure you use Google, Bing, or other credible search engines.

"You Weren't Arrested; You Were Rescued!"

That's what my friend Carmen told me two days before I started my last bid. Carmen Warner-Robbins (yes, that's her last name, and she wasn't named after the Air Force base) runs a prisoner reentry program called Welcome Home, San Diego. Some years ago, she gave up her position as a professor of emergency room nursing to devote her full-time efforts to assisting women coming home from prison to the San Diego area. Hundreds of women have made the successful transition back home because of the work of Carmen and her staff. So, when she speaks about how to do a bid, I listen.

"You weren't arrested; you were rescued," she said, squeezing my face and chin like only your grandma or auntie can do when they want your attention. That was the beginning of my learning to think differently about my incarceration in ways that give me hope that I never have to go through that again.

Carmen was making a point. At a certain level, it doesn't matter if you are guilty or innocent. The question she wanted me to answer was, If you hadn't been arrested that night, where would you be now? Where was your life headed?

I preached a sermon on that subject at the Iowa Women's Prison a couple of years after I got out. When I announced,

"I wasn't arrested; I was rescued," the place erupted like an Oprah Winfrey show with her saying, "You get a car, and you get a car, and you get a car!" Afterward, I talked to the minister about it, and she said, "I counsel these women all the time. Most of them believe that if they had not been arrested, they would be dead by now."

You will never hear me say I am glad I went to jail, but I have had to use that experience as a catalyst for change since it happened. I would probably be dead or have killed someone by now. So, having a sense of gratitude for even that lowly experience helps me make the changes I need to stay home and be productive. Even when friends, family, and the system don't want you to have a second (or third, or fourth) chance. Life (and for me, God) says you can start all over. After all, you weren't arrested; you were rescued.

Questions for Reflections:
1. What does it mean to you to say, "I was not arrested; I was rescued!"? How does this phrase relate to you personally?

2. How were you rescued? What were the circumstances surrounding your rescue?

3. What are you going to do with the insight that you have gained from this experience?

4. How will you use the learned experience to help you today, tomorrow, and in the future?

5. How can you share this insight you gained with others who have a shared history?

6. How can you use this newfound revelation to help you as you move forward in your transformation process?

7. What will be the next steps you take?

Who Do You Think You Are?

What you think of yourself is more important than what others think of you.

I learned that in jail.

One of the other inmates saw me depressed about being incarcerated. He was clearly the leader on our block. He was doing a short bid on an old charge but had clearly turned things around with his family, he was working a good job (we were on a series of 15 weekends to satisfy a 30-day sentence), and he was looking out for all of us.

"OG, you ain't a bad guy. You just a good guy who messed up."

He didn't say "messed," but I am a preacher who limits quoting words that rhyme with "duck."

He was telling me to look at myself positively and my mistakes as correctable.

How do you look at you, yourself?

Several years ago, Tucker Carlson, a reporter at Fox News, interviewed Ashley Bell of the 20/20 Coalition about #BlackLivesMatter and said that the black community was better off with mass incarceration because it reduces crime rates. That's garbage because there is no statistical correlation between crime rates, incarceration, and public safety. On a personal note, the question is whether my family and friends were better off without me. The answer to that question is the "me" without whom they would be better off.

There were times in my life when my kids didn't want me around, but they weren't better off. They are better off not because their father went to jail, but because he sees himself differently from the Tucker Carlsons who misinterpret crime statistics.

Who do your kids need you to be? Who have others said that you are? Who are you?

As for me, I'm a good guy who messed up, and I will not be defined by my mistakes.

Questions for Reflections:

1. Before you can help others, you need to know who you are. Start with asking yourself, *Who do I think I am?* Now, who are you?

2. In comparing yourself to who you are and who others say that you are, which one of you do you like best? Why? Which one of you feels right to you?

3. If neither one feels right, how can you change your self-perception?

4. How do you evaluate or look at yourself? (Tip: Be objective in your review. In other words, use the same measuring tools on yourself as you would others.)

5. Write down those attitudes, characters, and actions you like and those you don't like about yourself in a separate column. Speak to a trusted friend, confidante, mentor, or therapist, and ask that person how you can develop positive habits. Then find articles to read that will assist you in making the appropriate changes.

6. Ask yourself, *What am I learning?* Keep a daily journal of your progress and setbacks.

7. It is essential to ascertain how you learn. Do you learn best through visual observation, hearing, or touching? Or do you learn best by combining two or all three of these ways?

Speaking of Addiction . . .

America is addicted to mass incarceration. It is just the latest drug of choice in a series of binges designed to keep a permanent hold of social control over people like us. That's the conclusion I drew after reading "The Black Family in the Age of Mass Incarceration," Ta-Nehisi Coates's timeless essay in *The Atlantic*.

This country can't get enough. Coates moves through America's methods of getting high on control, from slavery, through segregation, through discrimination, through lynching, into the failed War on Drugs and mass incarceration. He talks about the impact of incarceration on families left behind—your family does your bid with you—the financial strain; the dashed hopes; and the pain of separation. Even when a brother is trying to get right, the system finds ways to maintain control. Sounds like a dope fiend, doesn't it?

Those of us committed to our recovery from addiction know all too well that a sure way to sabotage getting clean and sober is to try to do it without changing other facets of life, such as people, places, and things. We had to change our thinking, and some of us "came for the drinking and stayed for the thinking."

Coates's piece concludes with a similar prescription for America's addiction. "It is not possible to truly reform our justice system without reforming the institutional structures, the communities, and the politics that surround it."[1] People who want to get rid of mass incarceration will have to invest in education; employment; investments in poor neighborhoods; and, I would add, meaningful alternatives to deal with behaviors that have been deemed criminal. Getting rid of mass incarceration without wholesale investment in the communities most affected is like getting clean and sober without changing people, places, and things. I am staying sober one day at a time and committed to freeing America of its addiction.

Questions for Reflections:
1. What is the following Coates statement saying to you? "It is not possible to truly reform our justice system without reforming the institutional structures, the communities, and the politics that surround it."

2. In which areas are you interested in pursuing change, institutional structures, the community, or the politics surrounding needed reforms?

3. How are you committed to being sober to be part of the solution and not the problem?

4. If you are committed to being part of the solution, how can you help your family?

5. If you aren't ready to be part of the solution, are you willing to seek help for yourself?

6. In what ways can you help advance positive change in your community?

7. In what ways can you help improve the institutional structures and/or the politics surrounding them?

[1]"The Black Family in the Age of Mass Incarceration," by Ta-Nehisi Coates, *The Atlantic* (October 2015).

We Have a Voice, Ya' Heard?

There's a story about a couple of guys who were talking about their problems back in the day. One was flat broke. He asked his friend for a loan. His friend replied, "I'll lend you money when the president is black, and the Pope is latino."

I hope dude got his boy's phone number back in 2016.

Things changed that we never thought we'd see, and one of them is that people like popes and presidents are listening to us. And if so, it's about time.

The Pope seems to be listening. He visited Curran-Fromhold Correctional Facility in Philadelphia that year. The president that year seemed to be listening to us when he visited El Reno Federal Prison. Excerpts from his visit aired on the Vice network. President Barack Obama opened his conversation with El Reno residents by telling them he was interested in reforming the system and developing stronger supports for those coming home from jail and prison. He had gone to El Reno, he said, because he wanted to hear their stories.

We all have stories about how we got to prison, what it was like, and what is happening now. What the president's interviews revealed was how our stories are not ours alone. Our families and friends, our sons and daughters, our mothers and fathers all feel the impact of our decisions. They also feel the impact of harsh, disproportionated sentences imposed on people of color, disparate policing policies in our neighborhoods (If you didn't see the show, a police officer talked about how they were supposed to police our neighborhoods differently and that middle-class white people would never let them get away with that. I hope he has insurance.), and politicians trying to win elections by being tough on crime. We are on our second president since then. We must make sure he listens.

President Obama's visit was designed to give us more visibility and shine a light on the human cost of what has gone wrong with our system of criminal (in)justice. And now that you're home—or once you get home—what will you do with the spotlight? Because even though you may not be the president or the Pope, you can use your voice to change the system, like the people I sat with the day after the Pope's visit and the president's TV show are working to ensure voting rights in Florida, or the guys I'll be working with around the country to mobilize for more reentry support systems. It's time for real talk when somebody's listening.

Questions for Reflection:
   1. Why is it important to share your story with someone?

   2. Are you prepared to be transparent (open and honest) with others in telling your story?

3. How can you spotlight the inequities of the justice system through the telling of your story?

4. How can you galvanize your family or circle of friends to help improve the lives of other returning citizens?

5. What decisions can you make that will positively impact your life for the better?

6. How will you get started on your quest to change yourself?

7. In being transparent, are you being true to yourself?

Your Life Has Value, No Matter What You Have Done

They can call you a thug, an animal, a predator—whatever—but your life has value. Even the Declaration of Independence says people are "endowed by their Creator with certain unalienable Rights, that among these are Life, Liberty and the pursuit of Happiness." And you are "people."

Kelly Gissendaner was executed in 2015 in Georgia. News outlets around the world publicized her killing. I heard it on British Broadcasting Corporation radio. So much has been made of this woman having turned her life around after being convicted of plotting the murder of her husband almost 20 years ago.

Gissendaner earned a certificate in theology from Emory University. Her children cried, wanting to see her sentence commuted to life without parole. I personally know women who served time with her. One publicly stated that Gissendaner saved her life while in prison, talking her out of suicide. Many point to these changes and say she should not have been executed.

I disagree. I acknowledge that she should not have been executed, but not because she had changed. After all, how much change is change? No, I believe that the death penalty is wrong because every life has value.

Suppose Gissendaner had been a brother and had no kids crying (that he knew of) for him, not only with no theology certificate, but without the ability to read or write. Suppose he had never talked another inmate out of suicide? His life still would have mattered. He still would have been God's creation; his life would have had value.

As we deal with our criminal pasts, the questions for us today are, Do we believe that about ourselves? Do we live as though our lives have value? Do we cherish the time on this planet to be people of purpose? And do we value the lives of others, irrespective of their past or present?

The system said that Gissendaner's life did not matter. But while on death row, she believed that not only did her life have value, but so did the inmate about to take her own life. Does life have value to you? Live like it on your bid and when you come home.

Questions for Reflections:

1. What does it mean to you that you have self-worth or that your life has value?

2. Take time to ponder before answering this question: What makes you unique?

3. There is an old saying, "If you always do what you've always done, you will always get what you've always got"? With that in mind, what are you doing differently so you know that your life matters if to no one else but you?

4. Make a list of what you would like to do to make a difference or positively impact someone else's life. Which item on your list will be your starting point?

5. Do you know where you stand or what you believe concerning the value of human life?

6. I read in the news that a man asked his friend for some of his French fries while riding in a car. When his friend told him jokingly, "No man, go buy your own," the man who wanted the French fries shot the other man in the back of the head and reached over to catch the fries! How can you help to change others' perception of the value of life?

7. When you realize that you are a precious creation of God, how do you feel?

Gotta Get Back on My Feet

Do you want to get back up? Reach for something higher. Reach for something bigger.

When I was on the yard, I had a ritual. While the young bulls played ball, I looked for grass growing between the cracks of cement. First, I couldn't ball if you put me in the paint with a stepladder. But, second, I needed a reminder that the walls and wire did not confine nor define me. So the grass breaking through reminded me that there is something bigger.

That's what I thought about in 2015 when I listened to Glenn Martin from JustLeadershipUSA (https://www.justleadership usa.org/) talk about his move from a six-year bid to forming a corporation. That's what struck me when I sat on a panel with Jondhi Harrell that day, discussing the role that we, as return- ing citizens (not ex-offenders; I refuse to be defined by my past), should play in supporting those coming home through orga- nizations such as The Center for Returning Citizens. (www. tcrcphilly.org).

Listening to Five Mualimm-ak of The Incarcerated Nation (http://www.incarceratednation.org/), I thought we can make a difference in the policies and practices of those coming behind us. Pastor Chris Kimmenez challenges me every time I think about his rise from dope dealer to director of training of Healing

Communities USA (www.healingcommunitiesusa.com). They all did serious time, and they all reached for something bigger.

You may be focused on just getting things right for yourself or yourself and your family. But if this country is going to change from its current focus on locking people up instead of making people better, it is going to take you, us, to do it. That's why Glenn Martin says, "Those closest to the solution are those closest to the problem." You, and something bigger than you, got you into this. Now it will take you and something bigger than you for a solution.

One thing bigger than you is each organization listed above. They all look for members, volunteers, and supporters to build a movement that seeks solutions to mass incarceration. Just about every area has someone like them committed to you and those coming behind. A movement—can you see it? That's something bigger than you. And while you are focusing on your situation, take time to envision your role in it.

Yes, I'm a preacher, and I know God is bigger than me. But I also know that God uses movements (churches, masjids, temples) to bring about change. All of it is about knowing there is something bigger, better, higher. Next time you're thinking about getting back on your feet—for that matter, next time you're ballin'—stop for a second, and find some blades of grass.

Questions for Reflections:
　1. What does it mean to you to be a team player?

　2. How do you work best: alone or with others?

3. Do you respect others because they think or look differently than you?

4. In deciding to help make a difference in your life, as well as the lives of others, what do you believe are the positive characteristics that you can bring to the table in helping to improve the lives of re-entering citizens or to change the popular sentiment legislators have toward mass incarceration?

5. What skills do you possess or can gain to make a difference in your life experience toward joining the fight to eliminate mass incarceration?

6. What skills do you possess or plan to learn to help improve the lives of re-entering citizens?

7. The author used a blade of grass as a symbol of hope for a better future. As you move forward with your life, having read this devotional, what small something reminds you that you have hope?

I'm a Shareholder

That's how my man introduced himself from the podium at a fundraiser breakfast. The organization having the breakfast provides support groups called for men and women returning home from jail or prison. Sometimes, you need someone to talk to about the transition home. Yes, I know sometimes you want to keep it bottled up, but that makes it worse. We weren't born to be alone; otherwise, we'd be trees or something like that.

Every human being that comes into the world comes through another human being and by a second human being. That makes three of y'all, unless somebody runs (and it ain't you). So even when you say you don't need anybody, you are lying to yourself. Have you ever told somebody you don't need anybody? Ha! You needed them to hear that!

So you need someone to talk with, someone who can keep it real, someone who understands, someone who will listen and not just give a bunch of advice as if you're stupid. Research says that having good relationships is more significant in keeping you home after a bid than getting a job.

That's what dude was raising money for when he said, "I'm a shareholder."

A shareholder is part owner of a company. A shareholder buys stock in a company, invests, and when the company makes money, some of it comes back to him or her. One of my running buddies was a shareholder in a pharmaceutical firm, except he didn't make initial investments before he collected. No, this is different.

This shareholder at breakfast talked about how he, his church, and some other brothers bought stock in a prison company, Corrections Corporation of America. You probably knew that some prisons are being run now by corporations that contract with the government to run prisons or jails for them, and they get paid big-time based on how many beds they fill. The more arrests and convictions, the more money they make. That's messed up, somebody making cash on your misery.

But that's not why my man became a shareholder. He did it because he and his support circle not only talk to one another, they act. Sometimes you gotta get past the talk and walk the walk. They realized that part of their trauma in coming back home was that they were housed in facilities where the bottom line was the bottom line, not rehabilitation or anything like that. So the church buys stock so the shareholders can go to meetings, tell other people who make money off their misery what a bid is like, and talk about what we should be doing when a person makes a mistake instead of collecting and warehousing them for a fee.

They support one another; they reach back for the next generation. And that's an enterprise in which we can all be shareholders.

Questions for Reflections:
1. What meaning does the word *shareholder* take on for you?

2. Are you interested in becoming a shareholder in a company or corporation to help others while stabilizing yourself financially? If so, what kind of business?

3. For instance, one person started his own baking company and hires others who are returning citizens. How would you go about helping others?

4. Have you thought about preparing a business plan for your new enterprise?

5. Make sure you reach out to the Small Business Administration regional office for guidance. Also, check with them for local resources.

6. Where would you seek funding for your business(es)?

7. How would you go about seeking reputable firms suitable for investing? Make one of your first stops at the public library.

It's a Rainy Night in Georgia

You may not be old enough to remember Brooke Benton's soul song "It's a Rainy Night in Georgia," but I am. I won't tell you how old I am, but the first time somebody called me Pop-Pop, it was a CO leading me to the nurse after I passed out in a holding cell with 70 other guys serving 30-day sentences on 15 weekends. But I digress.

I have been spending a lot of rainy nights in Georgia because I am providing training to houses of worship all over the state that have decided they want to be places that welcome home men and women from prisons and jails. Since last year, I have spoken with hundreds of religious leaders on behalf of my organization, Healing Communities USA, about being ready to receive, support, and empower what we call "returning citizens," a more hopeful term than *ex-offenders*.

We have talked about supporting families of incarcerated men and women, supporting people coming home, even helping crime survivors develop a sense of healing and forgiveness. When I've gone to bed on those rainy nights in Georgia, I was exhausted from the conversations about how the faith community (Christian, Jewish, Muslim, and others) can be there for people coming home.

Other states have similar initiatives. They recognize that thousands of people come to worship every Sunday, every

Saturday, every Friday, burdened by their struggles associated with their son, daughter, grandchild, sibling, or parent locked up in the system. They want support, and they want to help.

My organization, HCUSA, has been working with state governments, departments of corrections, churches, masjids, and temples to help them get ready for people coming home, the families left behind, and people struggling with having been crime victims. We have had these conversations and trainings from Montana to Florida, Massachusetts to California. We are finding people that want to help.

This is a sign of hope that those of us who come through the criminal justice system have not been abandoned. We just need to connect with the people we can trust and want to help. Not just people who want to feel good about themselves because they are "lending a hand."

We are doing two things: First, we are talking to currently and formerly incarcerated people to see if they have family in a house of worship so we can contact that church, masjid, synagogue, or temple to help them reconnect. Second, we provide training so they'll know how to love and support us, not just do us a favor so they'll feel good about themselves.

Soon, I will head back to the South and the rain. People hate rain because it's inconvenient. Whenever it rains, I think about how many of us won't get yard that day. And when it's lightning and thundering, I remember how many of us got lockdown. So on my next rainy night in Georgia, I will pray for people who are more than inconvenienced and walk through the rain to the next training meeting.

Questions for Reflections:

1. After hearing the author's version of a rainy night in Georgia, understanding that these are long, arduous days and nights working to secure improved conditions for returning citizens, families of the left behind, and victims of crimes, what does your rainy night in Georgia look like?

2. How do you plan to connect with people you trust or seek to help?

3. How do you visualize yourself as an ex-offender or a returning citizen? Why? In your mind's eye, how are the images differing from you?

4. In connecting with a faith organization or a place of worship, what would substantial assistance look like to you?

5. Have you thought about getting in touch with local pastors to get involved in their programs to help others?

6. How will you seek help to better sensitize yourself to the plight of those inmates with different issues from yours who are yet to return home?

7. Have you thought about what specialized training you might need or what area you want to pursue in helping others, for example, peer counseling?

Despising Shame

We didn't have chapel services in the unit where I was housed in jail. The chaplain never came on the block either. So we started our own service.

The best sermon I heard in jail was from my cellie. He talked about how Jesus, while incarcerated, "despised the shame" of it. He explained that although others were ashamed of him for being arrested, Jesus would not let his arrest, imprisonment, or execution define him. And in the end, he was vindicated. (Christians call that the Resurrection.)

I thought about that sermon while remembering my shame and how I had to get over it and make my time productive. As long as I wallowed in shame, I allowed my brain to be preoccupied with anger and pity. But when I learned to despise the shame, I could focus on making the mental changes necessary to succeed when the bid was over.

We have to despise the shame. Shame is paralyzing and unproductive. Besides, enough people are trying to shame us that we don't need to give them any help. Even church people who believe in Jesus play the shame game. One of my students, studying to be a minister at Howard University, tried to play the shame game with me, She said she didn't like incarcerated people because they are horrible. She called us "those people."

"Well, if you don't like those people, let me borrow your Bible," I said. When she asked why, I told her, "We have to take some things out. If you don't like those people, we have to get rid of the Book of Genesis because Joseph was locked up. If you don't like those people, you have to eliminate the Book of Jeremiah because he was in solitary confinement. If you don't like those people, you have to tear out the Book of Daniel because he was a two-time loser; and Shadrach, Meshach, and Abednego were on death row.

"If you don't like those people, there goes the Book of Revelation, since John wrote that while he was locked up. Get rid of First and Second Peter because he got popped. And while the church prayed for him all night long, when he got an early release, Peter came back to the church, and they wouldn't let him in, so things haven't changed. If you don't like those people, stop saying 'I can do all things through Christ who strengthens me,' because a man in a Roman jail wrote it."

Someone tried to point out that those were all "good people" incarcerated for their faith. I countered by pointing out that Moses killed an Egyptian, David conspired to have his baby mama's husband murdered, and Paul was an accessory to murder in the killing of Stephen. And Peter would have been killed by police after he attacked one of them when Jesus was arrested. Yet God used them all for positive purposes.

If you are wrestling with shame today, tell that committee in your head that they're fired. You were built for positive purposes with divine destiny. So you took a detour on your way. Despise the shame, and stake your claim on the road to a positive destiny.

Questions for Reflections:

1. Are you experiencing feelings of self-pity and shame due to being incarcerated? If so, why? Note: It is imperative to get in touch with your feelings and understand why before you can start the process of moving on or beyond the pain and shame. Describe it; then deal with it and let it go!

2. What does the author mean by "despising shame"? Ponder it, look up the definitions of the two words, and then write down how it relates to your situation? If you are a Bible-believing person, or even if you are not, I would ask you to read the stories mentioned above from the Bible to draw your perspective of what "despising shame" means to you. Deal with it, question it within yourself, and then put your thoughts on paper.

3. Why is it essential for you to despise the shame, as the author states in the above devotional?

4. What ways can you put despising the shame to good use in your life for the benefit of others and you?

5. Now that you have fired the negative self-talk, it is time to seek God for guidance as to your divine destiny. To do this, it is time to map out a plan. What elements are vital for you to list to find your positive purpose in life?

6. Knowing that it is crucial to have positive and productive people that you can trust to assist you in the process, who will you seek assistance to help you on your journey to your newfound purpose?

7. What ideas come to mind as you journey your new path for purpose?

Stopping the Curse

You have probably never heard of Yasmine Arrington, but she could be your daughter—or in my case, granddaughter. She represents our children, the children of the incarcerated, who are the most at-risk of becoming incarcerated themselves by popular wisdom.

But not Lady Yaz.

Yasmine, a first-year student at Howard University School of Divinity, is the founder and CEO of ScholarChips. This not-for-profit organization provides college scholarships for the children of the incarcerated because she is one herself.

"My father and I were out of touch from the time I was three years old until I was around fourteen or fifteen," said the articulate honors graduate of Elon College in North Carolina. "But then we started writing. And when I got to college, we were able to see each other."

I asked Yasmine how she felt about her father, who is still incarcerated, part of the churn in and out of jail. "I have forgiven him," she said, referring to his physical absence from her life. "I grew up in church, gave my life to Christ at an early age, and it was instilled in me to forgive. I hold no grudge. Life is too short and precious for me to hold on to anger. Grudges can be debilitating, and I want to set an example for the young people in our program."

And she has inspired many young people. They attend colleges from Penn State to Bowie State, from Spelman to Towson, from Alabama State to Virginia State, from community colleges to Virginia Wesleyan.

It has been "difficult to keep an ongoing relationship with her father's church," but she presses on. "I know he loves me," says the young social entrepreneur, but she would like a more "regular relationship." Yasmine went on to talk about how her father feels remorse, but that is "basically when he is behind bars again." That's a wake-up call for us all. The remorse we feel when incarcerated should be memorized and called up when we feel like doing something stupid again.

I thought about Yasmine one day when I was at a conference on mass incarceration sponsored by the Pennsylvania Council of Churches. During a break, I talked with Jondhi Harrell of The Center for Returning Citizens. We talked about the dire predictions for our kids. He has five; I have three. They are all doing well. They help us.

Yasmine told me how she encourages her father when he slides into pity parties and feels as if nobody loves him. She reminds him that he's a grown man and that he has to be responsible for his decisions. (Ouch! My daughter says the same to me.) "I don't know if he knows how to break the cycle," she said of his continued bids. But her encouragement is instructive to us all.

We are grown men (grown-a$$ men) who can thrive when we put our minds to it. Our children, like Yasmine, believe we can. And when they don't, we can prove to them otherwise. We can do it. Yasmine believes in us.

Questions for Reflections:

1. Are you a parent, aunt, uncle, big brother, big sister, or someone whom a child looks up to or loves greatly? If so,

describe this young person and how his or her unconditional love makes you feel?

2. How can you turn your feelings of remorse into positive preemptive actions instead of aftermath negative pity and remorse?

3. Think about some of the ways you can begin to be proactive in averting doing "something stupid," as the author so aptly puts it.

4. What does it mean to you to be a grown man or a grown woman?

5. Now that you have pondered proactive ways to avert doing something stupid, what are some of the actions and habits you have created in your mind that you can do? Note: It is vital to list them in your journal.

6. Part of being a grown man or a grown woman is accepting responsibility for your actions. In what ways will you take responsibility for your wrong actions and use your acknowledgment of the same to be a positive force in your life and the lives of those who love you?

7. How will you share the benefits of what you have learned to help others?

On April 3, 2015, Anthony Ray Hinton Came Home

After 30 years.

On death row.

For a crime, he didn't commit.

And the state of Alabama was aware since 1999.

Hinton's release was secured through the legal efforts of the Equal Justice Initiative (EJI) led by attorney Bryan Stevenson. EJI represents inmates wrongly and harshly convicted, including children sentenced to life without parole (what Stevenson calls "death-in-prison" sentences) and others who can't afford representation and suffer at the hands of an inhumane system.

How did Hinton survive? "My sense of humor," he told an audience of 40 religious leaders gathered for a two-day retreat at EJI's headquarters in Montgomery, Alabama. He used his imagination. "They took my freedom, but they didn't take my soul," he told us. "I got more frequent flier miles than anyone. In my mind, I even flew to England to have tea with the queen."

Hinton talked about his faith and his steadfast belief in God. He was released on Good Friday 2015, declaring, "The sun does shine," which became the title of his memoir. He went to church that Easter Sunday. His character is featured as the man in the cell next to Jamie Foxx in *Just Mercy*.

But the challenges of reentry still haunts him. He wakes up every morning at 3:00 AM for breakfast, just like he did when he was on death row. He has a king-size California bed, but he sleeps curled up as if he were still on a short cot in that 5-by-7 cell where he spent 30 years. "I can't stretch out!" he said, dabbing tears from his eyes.

But Hinton has support from EJI and others. He tells his story across the nation to show how the criminal justice system can misfire and repeat the legacy of slavery, lynching, and discrimination through wrongful convictions, inhumane treatment, and corrupt policies and politicians.

But I took away something else as well. Hinton said, "They didn't take my soul." The system can do that, but you also may have friends who want to take away your soul by getting you back into the foolishness that got you locked up in the first place.

Hinton's faith and internal strength made him strong enough to keep his soul. Even the COs on death row noticed. They repeatedly asked Stevenson, "When are you gonna get Mr. Hinton out of here?" When you keep your soul, integrity, and faith, even the people who want to or are charged to take it will notice. Guard your soul against all who would take you down a destructive path. And like Anthony Ray Hinton, you will be able to say, "The sun does shine."

Questions for Reflection:

1. What do you suppose Anthony Ray Hinton meant when he said, "They took my freedom, but they didn't take my soul? What positive effect does this statement have on you and your self-worth?

2. How do you think Mr. Hinton's sense of humor kept his jailers from robbing him of his sanity and his senses? How can you use such humor techniques to keep you fit for the struggles you are encountering now, whether you are a soon-to-be returning citizen or already a returning citizen?

3. Understanding that humor or comedy is not downplaying or making light of your situation but is another way of seeing the best of a bad situation, how have you used humor to improve your lot?

4. Have you ever imagined yourself elsewhere as Anthony Ray Hinton did on faraway travels during extremely trying times of your life? How did this technique help you cope with your struggles or difficulties?

5. What significance does Hinton's statement upon his release on Good Friday 2015, "The sun does shine," hold for you as a Christian or as a non-Christian?

6. The author cites, "Hinton's faith and internal strength made him strong enough to keep his soul. Even the COs on death row noticed." In whom or in what does your faith lie? Can you rely on, trust, and know that you will make it with the help of God? Why or why not?

7. Is this not another form of "faithing it until you make it"? If so, how?

Understanding the Process

"Has your address changed?"

"Has your phone number changed?"

"Has your cell phone number changed?"

"Have you missed any court-ordered payments?"

"Have you missed any court-appointed counseling sessions?"

"Have you had any contact with law enforcement or been arrested?"

That's what I had to answer for my PO.

When I got down to six months left until I got off paper, I was on internet reporting. Same questions, then hit "Submit." Yes, probation and parole have found a new use for the term *submit*. It also costs more money.

Probation and parole were not always viewed in negative terms. The people who didn't like probation and parole when they were started were jailers and police. The system didn't even start probation. A Boston shoe repairman named John Augustus came up with the idea in 1841, when he convinced the court to release a drunk into his care instead of sending the dude to prison. His work to get the man straight was successful, and he took on other people and started working with youth a few years later. His goal was always to help the person make a turnaround. Later his vision became part of the system, but not always with the same intention.

Parole was started by Alexander Maconochie in an English penal colony (a whole island that serves as a prison/jail, similar to Riker's) at Norfolk Island, 1,000 miles off the coast of Australia. He believed that if you gave people indefinite sentences and then gave them time to earn good time through work, study, and behavior, you could release them based on progress. The word *parole* comes from the French language for "word" because a parolee honored his word by good behavior. (I would have trouble saying "parole up, bruh.")

The probation and parole systems weren't designed to be against the client; they were there to help. It wasn't supposed to be "tail 'em, nail 'em, and jail 'em." And there are efforts around the country in places such as New York and Georgia to return to that sense of helping and providing hope. In the original parole system, even cops helped you find a job.

Meanwhile, there are good POs and not-so-good POs. Either way, I have to submit (the first way they meant it) to the system. Compliance is a better word, but sometimes it can feel like submission. And when it does, I try to take responsibility for my actions, do what I'm supposed to, and thank God I've had POs who were good.

Because I knew this too would pass, and I surrounded myself with people who supported the positive changes in my life, I could bounce frustrations off of them, knowing they would not tell me to do something stupid like not show up, or not hit "submit" on my e-form. And I am now part of that process started by Augustus and Maconochie, and I work for the good of those coming home behind me.

Questions for Reflection:

1. Why is it vital for you to internalize the six questions at the beginning of this chapter? What prominence does he purport

to them in his successful growth? What significance might
they have on your growth?

2. Do you think the parole system as it was intended is better
than the form it has evolved to today? Why or why not?

3. Have you been paroled for a violation that you committed
or given early release? If so, did you see it as a form of mercy?
If yes, how did you use the time wisely to benefit yourself or
others?

3. Do you think the probation system as it was intended is
better than the operational version functioning today? Why
or why not?

4. Have you ever been placed on probation instead of serving
the bid? If so, did you see it as a blessing and another opportunity of divine intervention, or did you perceive it to be luck?
What did you do that helped you on the road to recovery,
or did you squander the gift and wind up back in court or
prison?

5. What knowledge can you draw from the brief discussion on the good and bad POs? How can you positively put to use your experiences with good POs versus bad POs?

6. Have you developed a circle of close friends where you can vent and discuss your struggles? Do you know people who will encourage you to keep the faith and keep moving forward in your quest for sobriety?

7. Someone once dropped a few words of wisdom on me. She said, "Faith it until you make it." How can you use this statement to benefit you with your challenges?

Everybody Deserves a Job

Finding work when you get home from a bid is a challenge. In an increasingly automated and computerized economy, many jobs for persons accustomed to working with their hands have been eliminated. Many jobs have gone overseas or to different parts of the country that have lower labor costs.

Every state has "collateral sanctions," restrictions on the types of jobs available to people with felony convictions or other criminal records. And more communities are passing "ban the box" legislation, which means removing the box on job applications to check if you have a record. But most personnel people can still ask your permission to do a background check once you get an interview.

One resident in a county jail told me, "If I don't get a job soon after I get out, I will have to go back to selling drugs. It's all I know how to do."

My response to him was, "Wrong answer on two counts. First, if you leave that as an option, you'll probably do it anyway. That's what happens with most people. It's called making a reservation. Second, let's edit your sentence. Take out one word: *drugs*. All you know how to do is *sell*."

Starting a business has become one of the most attractive options for people coming home from jail or prison. Entrepreneurship is the key to financial freedom whether you're selling household products or travel; driving for Uber or some other transportation company; or developing a business in extermination, crime scene cleanup, or residential contracting. Any of these businesses could give a man or a woman an opportunity to create a career, not just making money. Some of us are great salespeople; we just need the right product.

Several years ago, Hofstra University surveyed a group of New York State Correctional System residents and a group of entering business students on entrepreneurial intelligence. Guess which group scored higher? You got it, the residents of the prison system. So think about starting a business as a way of making the transition back home. Go online and look for some help in starting your own business. Or grab a copy of the book *Thinking Outside the Blocks*. There is help available, but it starts with your mindset.

Questions for Reflections:

1. When looking forward to re-entry into the workforce, why is it essential to change your mindset when contemplating employment opportunities?

2. The definition of *entrepreneurship* is "the activity of setting up a business or businesses with the hope of profit." In what areas do you consider yourself skilled, such as using your mind to develop a selling strategy for a product or using your hands to create one?

3. As a man or a woman in the transition home, what plans should you be making now to begin the process of solidifying your future company?

4. S.W.O.T. analysis is the mechanism of evaluating your strengths, weaknesses, opportunities, and threats for success in your future business. Have you seriously begun to consider and document yours for your future business?

5. Have you thought about what changes in your life you may need to make o increase your support system in pursuit of being an entrepreneur?

6. It is essential to give back as an active member of society. In what ways might you consider paying it forward through your future business?

7. Do you have a specific group of people that you are looking to help?

Your Next Decision

That's what Darren Ferguson said to me one Sunday between services at Mt. Carmel Baptist Church in Far Rockaway, Queens, New York, where Ferguson served as pastor. It's a long way from where we met when I was teaching at Sing Sing prison, and Darren was an inmate.

Ferguson made some "next decisions" while serving an 8½-to-20-year bid for second-degree attempted murder. Ferguson prayed for the first time, he became a Christian, and he became a preacher. He went back to school and earned his college degree and numerous certificates. Today, Ferguson is a pastor and a deputy police chief for community affairs in Orange, New Jersey. He has an earned doctorate. You can call him doctor, bishop, professor, reverend, and pastor; but he chooses to be defined by his next decision.

How did he make the change?

"I went into prison a liability who thought he was an asset," he says. "I was too addicted to know I was a liability. My daughter changed that." Knowing that he had a toddler at home who needed her daddy, he decided to make a change. While at Sing Sing, he made a promise to his daughter to change.

"But people make promises to change all the time," I told him. "How did you keep your promise?"

"Fear," Ferguson said. "First, I feared God. The Bible says that after you are delivered from your demons, if you don't replace your past actions with new decisions, the demons come back seven times worse. I ain't wanting that.

"Second, my daughter needed me, and I wanted my family to be proud of me." Ferguson spoke of how his family's support was a major part of his successful return to society. But then I asked about people who don't have family support.

"Find something to motivate you, something you would fight for. You fought on the streets, so find something positive to fight for." He went on to say that life is a fight, and the fight of the streets is more brutal today than when he was out there 30 years ago. "There is still fast money out there," he said, "but no easy money. It ain't free-flowing like it was back in the day. I remember going to dudes' cribs, and they'd pull out money in garbage bags, sorted into tens, twenties, fifties, and hundreds. There's still folk making money out there, but not on the streets like it used to be."

It was almost time to go back to the sanctuary for the second service. The church was packed for the afternoon celebration, a recognition of Ferguson's fifty-second birthday, a long way from Sing Sing, but close enough that several men who did bids with him are members of the church now. I asked him how it feels—given his past, his imprisonment, the realization that his life caused pain and suffering—to be on this side of his life?

"You are not your past," he said, rehearsing a general mantra for all of us trying to start over. Then he made it personal. "I am greater than the sum of my parts."

That's what helps us all make "the next decision."

Questions for Reflection:

1. Why do you think the author so aptly titled this chapter "The Thing That Defines You the Most Is Your Next Decision"?

2. What do you need to do or change in your life to be defined by your next decision?

3. Have you made a list in your journal that sets down what you are doing, which are liabilities to success in life, and those habits and behaviors that are assets to having a productive life?

4. What replacement decisions can you make in your life that will please God and help yourself?

5. Take time to meditate on what motivates you to live a healthy, constructive, and fulfilling life. Do you have someone or something present in your life worth fighting "the good fight" through positive actions?

6. If you knew you only had six months or less to live, what would you want your legacy or other memories of you to be?

7. What makes you better or greater than the sum of your parts?

I Wished I Could Be One of Them

Tears streamed down her face as she addressed the audience gathered to support the expansion of college availability to incarcerated men and women and those who come home from prison. Neatly dressed in a business suit, she said, "I asked God to help me. I didn't want to be on the streets anymore, and then I got arrested."

That struck a chord in me because three days prior to reporting to Delaware County Prison, a friend had told me, "You weren't arrested; you were rescued." And when I told that story at a chapel service in a state women's prison in the Midwest, the women hollered as if Oprah had given each of them a new car.

I asked the pastor of the prison church who had invited me to preach that day to explain the outburst. "You just told their story," she replied. "So many women here started their journey here in abusive relationships, whether as children or grown women. They self-medicated with drugs and alcohol to cope and then found themselves in a lifestyle from which there seemed to be no escape. They believe that their cries to God for deliverance came in the form of their arrest."

Back to the woman in the business suit.

"I'd be coming home as the sun rose up and see people going to work. I wished I could be one of them."

The women in that Midwestern prison knew the feeling.
I could relate as well, remembering what it was like to hang out
in front of the 7-11 at 5:50 AM, waiting for them to open the
wine case at 6:00, while others were getting their morning coffee.
I wanted to be normal, too. I was tired of that life. But I needed
help and support to get out of it.

I know today that I will never be what society calls normal.
Those of us with addictions or addiction histories will never be
normal. Those of us with criminal records will never be considered normal. But we are human beings with hopes and aspirations just waiting for the chance to change, even though we don't
know where it will come from. Sometimes it is an emergency
room; sometimes a jail or a prison cell; sometimes an addictions
treatment center; sometimes an AA or NA meeting; sometimes
a church, mosque, or temple; sometimes an intervention from
family or friends.

But there is something within all of us that wants it. That's
what came up for that woman who "wished she could be one of
them." It's what came up for me watching people get coffee at the
7-11 and what has come up for you in moments of clarity when
your spirit and soul cried out for change.

Those women at the prison believed that God had answered
their prayers having them arrested and sent to prison. They took
the pain of confinement as an opportunity for change. I wish there
were more readily available opportunities for rescue besides a
correctional facility that may or may not assist in the transformation. I wish churches could be that. But, first, I have to agree
with the yearning of my soul that change is possible.

I have to believe that I can be productive and purposeful.
I can be resourceful and live in recovery. I can be a solid citizen,
family member, and friend. I can see that, as it says in the book
Alcoholics Anonymous, "No matter how far down the scale we

have fallen, our experience can benefit others."[1] That is why we all need communities of support and support groups that can help us transition back home.

We can establish a new normal of healthy self-esteem and healthy relationships with the support of healthy people. My addiction and record may never make me normal like the people getting coffee at the 7-11, but I can be an example of the power of divine transformation to those normal people who may not have even faced their demons. Besides, I don't know how many of those people getting coffee or going to work have experiences similar to mine in addiction and/or incarceration. I'm sure that some of the people we think are normal once stood on that woman's corner or in the parking lot of my 7-11 and wished for change as well.

Questions for Reflection:
  1. What is your "I'd be coming home as the sun rose up and see people going to work. I wished I could be one of them" moment?

  2. What happened when you experienced that moment?

  3. How did you feel when you experienced that moment?

  4. What does your new normal look like?

5. How are you purposeful and productive in your new normal?

6. Who are you sharing your struggles with as you navigate your new normal? Are you seeking aid and strength from a divine power? Who are you seeking help from as you adjust to your new normal?

7. Is helping others get to their new normal part of your plan? If yes, how? If no, why not?

[1]*Alcoholics Anonymous, Fourth Edition: The Official "Big Book" From Alcoholic Anonymous* (Alcoholics Anonymous World Services, Inc.; 4th edition, 2013); page 83.

What Is Going to Happen to My Children?

Such was a typical offering to my friend and colleague Sandra Barnhill during her time as a public defender. The women she represented wanted to know what would happen to their children while they were down. Over 30 years ago, it moved Barnhill to found ForeverFamily as a support and advocacy group for incarcerated women and their children.

I have talked with so many women about the strain of being separated from their children. I know many children with issues resulting from that separation. And I marvel at the resiliency of both groups because my kids were grown when I was locked up, and I can't imagine how my kids and I would have handled that.

Some programs, like ForeverFamily, Girl Scouts Behind Bars, and Philadelphia's Mommy Reads work diligently to keep parents in touch with their children. ForeverFamily takes children to visit their mothers and works to improve the environment of the visitation room to make it child-friendly. Girl Scouts Behind Bars helps mothers and their children stay connected through various crafts and projects. Mommy Reads donates books to the local jail and videotapes women reading to their children so they can take the recording to the child to hear their mothers read.

These programs hinge on the investment incarcerated women are willing to make in being active moms. They have not given up hope; you have not given up hope. They work to connect with their children despite the distance from home, the indifference of the system, and resentment from their children. They have not given up hope and neither should you.

I have seen women keep the connection. I have seen family reunions. I have seen healing take place between women and their children, beginning even during the bid, and sometimes long after. Time doesn't heal all wounds, but faith in a higher power, accepting life on life terms, and perseverance goes a long way. So, too, do those of us who are home who can work with the ForeverFamilies, Girl Scouts, and Mommy Reads of our communities.

The pain of separation cannot be denied, but neither can the hope of connection and reconnection. There are no hopeless people, but there are people without hope. Those of us who have hope can share it with others. It starts with listening to the pain. It begins with, "I will meet you where you are, but I will not leave you there!" It starts with a vision that mothers are destined to nurture and love, and walls and wires cannot overcome their witness.

Barnhill left her secure job as an attorney and created an organization that has kept hundreds of children connected with their mothers because she listened to her clients. Women from black sororities and church organizations collected books and tapes, and Girl Scout volunteers donated time and supplies. They believe in the power of motherhood unleashed and the healing of relationships.

"Ms. Sandy, what will happen to my children?"

We all have a say in that.

Questions for Reflection:

1. Sandy Barnhill sacrificed her profession to establish an organization to help children have positive contact with their incarcerated mothers. As a woman, what sacrifice are you willing to make to help mothers and children have positive connections and relationships?

2. My son, grandchildren, and great-grandchildren are the world to me, and I would do anything necessary to maintain meaningful contact with them. Do you have children? If so, what would you sacrifice to maintain a positive relationship with your children and grandchildren?

3. If you are a single woman, are you willing to step into unfamiliar territory and start mentoring children as they have no mother or relative who is the positive support in their life? If yes, when and through what agency? If not, think about it, why not? Didn't someone have a positive influence on your life? Shouldn't you give back?

4. What does the term *hopeless* mean to you? Why? Are you experiencing hopelessness? If so, ponder why and answer the question of why? What happened in your life causing you to feel hopeless?

5. What does the author mean by the statement, "There are no hopeless situations"?

6. The author speaks of looking to divine power to give you hope and deal with hopelessness. Are you ready to seek help from the divine source? If so, read the following versions of Psalm 46:1, 5, and 10 in the Bible. What are they saying to you? Do these verses offer you hope that someone is there for you, that this someone will help you, and that this someone is with you?

7. Do you believe in the significance of healing relationships? If so, what steps are you willing to take to help incarcerated mothers reconnect and develop positive relationships with their children?

"One Thing We All Adore Something Worth Dying for Nothing but Pain Stuck in This Game Searching for Fortune and Fame"

Tupac's words haunted me the day after hearing news of the death of David Bowie, British rock star, who's crossover hit "Fame" breathed that same spirit:

"Fame, makes a man take things over
Fame, lets him loose, hard to swallow
Fame, puts you there where things are hollow

"Fame, what you like is in the limo
Fame, what you get is no tomorrow
Fame, what you need you have to borrow."

Tupac said he's stuck. Bowie says there's no tomorrow. So why do we chase it? Why do we chase fame, cred, a name?

Read the lyrics above where both brothers talk about being what psychologists call "other-directed." Put simply, it matters to us more what other people think of us than what we think of ourselves.

I remember being in a group arguing about this when one dude screamed, "I don't care what none o'ya'll n****** think about me." Yes, he did care, because if he didn't, he wouldn't have said it. He wanted us to know he was independent, but he expressed it through depending on us to know it.

Get it?

What do you think of yourself? Do you believe in your worth, or do you depend on the opinions of others? Is what you like in the limo or your heart? Are you wrestling with "who controls our brain, who can [you] blame?"

The same newspaper that calls a black man in Missouri with a protest sign a thug, calls a white man with a gun in Oregon a protester. An employer calls you unemployable because of your record. Dudes on the street call you soft because you're trying to get out of the game, the hustle, and live a productive life for you and yours. But what do you think about you?

I opened one lecture in a class I teach at Howard University by pulling out a twenty-dollar bill. I asked the student, "Who wants i?" Everybody's hand went up. Then I crumpled up the bill. "Who still wants it?" I asked. Everybody's hand was still up. I threw it on the floor and stepped on it. Everybody still wanted it. I asked, "If I put it in the toilet, would you still want it?" Some hands went down, but one student said, "Maybe if it was a stack."

Do you know why they still wanted the money? Because even crumpled, dirty, stepped on, and dumped on, it never lost its value. It is what it is: a twenty, a fifty, a hundred, a stack—it has value. And you have more value within you despite your past. Stop chasing fame and all its pain. How others see you is far less important than how you see yourself. Fame ain't worth dying for. But you are worth living for.

Questions for Reflection:

1. Re-read the author's following recollection, "I remember being in a group arguing about this, when one dude screamed, 'I don't care what none o'ya'll n****** think about me.' Yes, he did care, because if he didn't, he wouldn't have said it. He wanted us to know he was independent, but he expressed it through depending on us to know it." What does that say to you about the person speaking?

2. What do you think of yourself? Or, simply put, what is your opinion of yourself? Do you value your life? Do you love and respect yourself? Why or why not??

3. Is what you like or want to be represented by the limo, or is what you like or want in your heart? Are you wrestling with "who controls your brain and who can you blame for your lot in life"?

4. Does it matter what others say about you, or does it bother you that others negatively generalize their comments about people who struggle with addictions or were imprisoned? If so, why do you allow their commitments to bother you?

5. How can you turn your hurt, anger, and pain into something positively directed to help you get beyond and over others' flawed depictions of you?

6. What can you do to demonstrate that you have more value within you despite your past?

7. As the author poses the following challenge to you, please take time to meditate on it. The statement directs you to "stop chasing fame and all its pain." Now that you understand how others see you is far less important than how you see yourself, what steps can you take to ensure that you don't fall back into the dark thinking that fame is more important than the consequences of your negative life actions?

A Lifetime "Stay Out of Jail" Pass

Story #1

Juan was short. His sentence was almost up. We were sitting in the day room in the county jail one evening. The subject turned to his upcoming plans for life after his release in a few months. "I really need a job," he said. "If I don't find one, I may have to go back to hustlin'. I mean, man, all I know how to do is sell drugs."

Story #2

Pete hadn't been thinking much about what he was going to do when he got home. One thing he was sure of: "I'm ditchin' my baby mama," Pete assured me. "I'm taking my daughter and finding another woman who don't use. As long as I'm around my baby mama, there's the temptation to use. Gonna find me a lady who don't get high, so I don't do that no more."

OK, time's up. These are both true stories. Did you locate the mistake in each story? If you missed the mistake, let me help you out. It's the mistake of drinking the "if" kool-aid.

In the first story, Juan has made hustling an option. *If* he doesn't find a job soon, he says he is going back to hustling. That means sooner or later, he will! Whenever we make something an option, we leave the door open to say it's all right to do, even when we know it's not. As long as it's an option, Juan might do it as an income supplement if he gets a job and it doesn't pay what he wants. Making anything an opportunity makes it a probability.

In the second story, Pete is making his recovery from addiction dependent on a new woman. *If* he finds a woman who is clean, he will stay clean. Now his recovery is dependent on someone else. He has handed over his ability to make decisions to someone else. He is other-directed, and *if* the new woman ever decides to use, Pete will be back in his addiction.

You got to drop the ifs.

It is an error to have hustling as an option if you want to go straight. It is a mistake to have your recovery depend on someone else. Ifs, options, and others will take you out. Make a decision about what you are going to do, and find people who support it, but it must be your decision.

By the way, Juan made another mistake. He said he only knows how to sell drugs. I disagree. He knows how to sell. He just had a bad product that got him popped. He can sell other things, from energy to Amway, to cellphone minutes to Traci Lynn products, or his interpretation of her motivational speeches using his life's examples. (Don't laugh. He won't get arrested.)

So I told you if you find the mistakes, you qualify for a "Stay Out of Jail" pass. That's right, if you find them and correct them for yourself. No ifs, ands, or buts.

Questions for Reflection:
1. In your mind, what does the author mean by the statement, "It's the mistake of drinking the 'if' kool-aid"?

2. Thoughtfully deliberate over the author's reasoning concerning the following statement, "Ifs, options, and others will take you out." Do you agree? Why or why not?

3. When the author says, "Make a decision as to what you are going to do, and find people who support it, but it must be your decision." Why is it so important that it must be your decision?

4. When something is your decision, you have the power or the ability in your hands, and the responsibility falls on you for the decisions made. Does this make you nervous or afraid? If so, why or why not?

5. What talents or skills make you unique? What talents or skills can you use to develop a trade that will positively benefit you and others?

6. What rewarding interest do you possess that would be helpful in positively propelling you toward your small business or patentable product or idea?

7. Have you found the mistakes in Stories #1 and #2? Are you identifying the errors in your life story? If so, you are well on the way to collecting your reward, of staying out of jail and staying clean!

Somebody Else Needs You

In an earlier chapter, I gave you a list of people who need you as we work to get rid of this biased, overbearing system of too many arrests, incarcerations, insufficient releases, and too many repeats that keeps us chained to forces that keep us down. We talked about organizations that are working for change and improvements. We discussed how those of us who have done time are essential to that change. Remember Glenn Martin's statement, "Those who are closest to the problem are the ones closest to the solution." We need you.

But somebody else needs you!

And that's you. You need you!

If you are going to be about changing this flawed system of incarceration and punishment, you will have to be fit for the journey—not perfect, just fit. As the old folks used to say, "Clothed and in your right mind."

The you that you need is not the rep you've built or the street cred you've earned. So much of that is the result of acting so that people will see you in a particular light. That has its place; your image is essential. But it ain't you. *You* are you.

"Who is you?" That's bad grammar, but it's good thinking. While sitting in a group in detox, I was asked that question while recovering from another run with the bottle. The counselor had us watch this video on self-esteem and self-definition.

"Look at *you!*" he practically shouted. "That ain't *you* sittin' there. It's the shell your drug of choice created! But somewhere inside that shell is the real *you*, and we are going to work to find it."

As I'm writing this on the train, we just passed a state prison. I wonder how many dudes in there have discovered their authentic selves. It's tough to be you in prison; you can get played, punked, or worse. But as Lennie Spitale, a veteran of serious time and later a prison volunteer, has told me, "In prison, even the toughest guy cries at least one night."

Underneath the rep and the cred beats a heart that is as normal as anyone. And to enter the struggle to straighten out this criminal justice system, we need to be fit. How can you be sick and change a sick system?

So for me, that means it's time to do another Fourth Step in recovery: list my resentments; my pain; and, most important, my role in causing it or putting myself in a position to be hurt because I was selfish in the first place (as in "She played me, hurt me, 'effed over' me, but I wanted to be with her in the first place because she made me look good"). Do that thoroughly, and ask someone I trust to give me feedback on when I've been self-centered, selfish, dishonest, manipulative, and so on. When were those times when I'd rather save my face than save my a$$ets and keep churchin' and perpetratin'? Then ask God, Allah, Jesus, something greater than me to remove those flaws so that the real me can shine.

That's my way. Yours may be different. But the truth remains: You need you to get things straight and enlist in this army that also needs you.

I read a book called *Crook County* by Nicole Gonzalez Van Cleve. It's about the corruption in the Cook County jail system. (That's Chicago, yo.) The incredible account of what's wrong with the system, from cops to DAs to PDs to the laws on the books. But two things are true. Not only is the system corrupt, but I am at my best in challenging that system when I am at my best. That means I need me. And you need you. Let's get fit and change this system.

Questions for Reflection:

1. The author unleashes his bitterness and resentments concerning the criminal justice system in the United States and his anger toward his past poor life decisions. Being honest with yourself, list your resentments, bitterness, and issues you are harboring concerning your incarceration and your experience with the criminal justice system. Now make a list of regrets concerning your poor life decisions.

2. Take your list of resentments, bitterness, and issues and ferret out which of these emotions and concerns are resulting from poor life decisions on your part. How can you address them and make changes to your behavior, characteristics, and habits?

3. Through your self-assessment, are you one who sees a half glass of water half empty (pessimism) or half full (optimism)?

4. Through your fit assessment, have you determined that you need the aid of a counselor, therapist; or can you, God, Allah, or Jesus work on your fitness level in partnership?

5. If you need to seek professional counseling or work with the divine power operating in your life, are you ready to do the work?

6. Looking at the list mentioned above, how can you address the problems in the criminal justice system?

7. Reviewing and meditating on both lists, what is one of the most important things you have learned about yourself and your experience through your quiet self-evaluation time?

Acting on Positive Messages

Fred sent me a video on Facebook a little while ago. It was a video of a man reciting poetry. I ain't much into poems, but Fred knew I would like this one.

I met Fred about five years ago. Good thing I didn't meet him 20 years ago. Back then, Fred was a cop in a Midwestern city, patrolling a beat where I hung out in my days of active alcoholism. If I had met Fred then, my jacket would be longer and lousier than it is now. But when I met Fred, it was in a university classroom. He was in the process of becoming Rev. Fred, and I was clearing the fog that had gotten in the way of Professor Harold Dean.

We found out in that classroom just how close our paths had come to crossing in my days of insanity. But we also discovered how close our vision had become to helping the young men and women on the streets we both walked, though for obviously different reasons.

That's why Fred knew I would like the poems. The young man (hey, to me, 40 is young) recited two poems, one to his mother and one to his son. Both poems looked back on his life and reflected his hope for the future. A 13-year bid had robbed him (turnabout fair play) of a major part of his life. Now, he reflected backward in his poem to his mom.

"I didn't listen," he said, "because I didn't think the man understood, but I was an adolescent inside of a man's body." His moms told him he wasn't a man yet, but "I didn't listen. I didn't think you knew nothin' about the streets."

Fred's regrets turned to lessons for his son. "Listen," he told his son in the second poem, "it's not the messenger who saves you; it's the *message!*" And for this brother, this warrior, "the message was Jesus," he declared to the church congregation in the video. This time, everybody was listening.

Jesus, Allah, Buddha, Jehovah—all carry a positive message. I'm not trying to convert you, but you need a message. We get hung up on messengers and miss the message, the message of an opportunity, another chance, the choice to take a different path. Many times, we feel the messenger has no cred and can't tell us anything. But the reality is a lot of us throw away the message because we don't trust any messenger but the voice in our heads, and to all others, "You can't tell me nothing."

But get honest for a moment. Aren't there some messages that you wish you had paid attention to? And like the brother in the video, do you have a message for the next generation? He wants to leave his son a positive legacy, to learn from the sins of the father. I don't want my sons following any of the destructive paths of my past. Rev. Fred wants to offer the young men and women more than cuffs and free transportation in a government vehicle. Despite our past—young, middle-aged, or old—we can listen today and have a word for the tomorrows of the next generation.

Questions for Reflection:
    1. "I didn't listen," he said, "because I didn't think the man understood, but I was an adolescent inside of a man's body." His moms told him he wasn't a man yet, so "I didn't listen. I didn't think you knew nothin' about the streets." As you look

back on your current or most recent bid, what is the dialogue between the man and his mother saying to you? Do you get what his mom was telling him? Why or why not?

2. How can you positively use his mom's advice to benefit your life as a returning citizen?

3. "Listen," he told his son in the second poem, "it's not the messenger who saves you; it's the *message!*" What is the message of the second poem saying to you? How does the life of Jesus (Jehovah) or the messages of Allah or Buddha help to impact your life decisions, actions, behaviors, habits, and attitude to benefit your lifestyle and ethic?

4. Why is it, as the author says, "many times, we feel the messenger has no cred and can't tell us anything"?

5. Think about some of the significant decisions you have made that landed you in a bid. Now list them and ask yourself what you can do differently as a returning citizen to ensure a changed outcome for your life's opportunities for achieving your new life goals?

6. How can these new goals aid you in assisting those young people's lives for the better?

7. In the following statement, the author proffers a challenge to you: "Despite our past, young, middle-aged or old, we can listen today and have a word for the tomorrows of the next generation." Are you ready to accept his challenge? If yes, what precisely will you do to help the tomorrows of the next generation? Do you have someone wise in your life whom you trust to provide you with a credible message?

It's Not All About Me

Like most active alcoholics and addicts, I had selfishly over-looked how my continual drinking or usage affected others. I thought I wasn't hurting anybody but myself. I had to learn, and am still learning, that what I did and what I do affects others. In rehab, I received letters—what they call "cost letters"—from family members detailing how they felt and how they experienced my drinking. My daughter said the worst day of her life was watching the police load me into the back of a patrol car in front of the house.

I am currently reflecting on how others experienced my incarceration as I mourn the loss of my mother-in-law. While I was in jail, she supported me, made sure I had clothes to wear when I qualified for work release, and welcomed me into her home when I was released. But she struggled with the shame associated with my incarceration.

"Why'd you have to tell them that?" she asked after I told my story of being a prisoner as part of a sermon at her church. "They don't need to know all that!" She struggled with the shame of having a formerly incarcerated son-in-law. Like many relatives, she felt it reflected on her, her daughter, and grandchildren. She never stopped loving or caring for me, but she was scarred, and I have to take ownership of that because my actions resulted from my selfishness—all about me.

But I do not take full responsibility for her shame. First, while I admit my part, our culture has a lot to do with causing this type of shame. We are labeled and dehumanized as inmates, called names, and sentenced to perpetual guilt. When we come home, we are told we have paid our debt to society, but labels such as *ex-con*, *ex-offender*, and such are the unpaid interest on the debt we never stop paying. Bryan Stevenson, of the Equal Justice Initiative, reminds us that no human being should be defined by their worst mistake.

And then, everyone's thoughts are indeed their own. While I couldn't change what she thought of my incarceration, I could live in a manner that would temper the shame by making better decisions on this side of the razor wire. And I can be, and am, grateful that she never stopped being a presence for me in the years since I got out. It's not all about me, and by making better decisions and working to change a culture that dehumanizes, overcriminalizes, and labels its citizens through systemic mass incarceration, I can make it better for others like my late mother-in-law, who loved amid the hurt. You now know what it is like to be free.

Questions for Reflection:

1. Do you feel that most things are about you and how you think? If so, why?

2. The author discusses what his daughter told him in the first paragraph, which helped him determine that he would not return? What happened to cause your determination not to do a return?

3. As the author reflects on how his incarceration experience affected the lives of his loved ones, are you doing any self-reflection as to your understanding and empathy or lack of empathy for loved ones? Have you thought about how they may still be struggling with the stigma of what they experienced as they loved and supported you during your bid?

4. Have you sat down with loved ones to give them a chance to discuss what they went through and how they have been scared as a result of their secondary exposure to your experience?

5. Do you believe that listening empathically to loved ones' feelings will help you and them to heal and move on? If yes, why? If no, why not?

6. Why is it important to understand the meaning of Bryan Stevenson's statement, "No human being should be defined by their worst mistake"?

7. How can you make a difference to better your life and the lives of those who love and support you by helping to change the system's culture that dehumanizes and overcriminalizes returning citizens like you?

My Granddaughter Got Me Thinking About a Man I Met in Court

I had sat in the courtroom in Newark, New Jersey, glad I was not the defendant this time. I was an observer and listened to a man reading from a yellow sheet of paper. He was about my age, and his hands shook as he read his composition for the judge. The subject was legacy.

The essay he had written was mandated by the Newark Community Court and an innovative partnership between the Newark Municipal Court and Newark Community Solutions. They treated each case much like a team of social workers, the assistant district attorney, the public defender's office, a social worker, probation officer, and the judge developing alternatives to incarceration for low-level, nonviolent offenders. The man reading before us was assigned to write an essay on the types of legacy he wanted to leave to his grandchildren.

Playing Head, Shoulders, Knees, and Toes with my granddaughter brought that man back to my mind. He stumbled through his emotional letter to his grandchildren, telling them how he wanted them to remember him as a good grandfather, good to his family, and a positive influence in the community.

Of course, it was his negative past bad decisions that got him in court in the first place. But here he was with an opportunity to turn his life around, and part of his sentence was to write this letter, to think about how he wanted to be remembered. I thought about him as I looked at my granddaughter.

I want her to remember the good Grandpop, fun to be with, and an asset to the community. I want her to be surprised when the day comes—and it will—that she finds out the reason she calls me Grandpop and not Granddad is that I need no extra reminders of my drinking days. I am living one day at a time so that she will never see me drunk, never know me as an incarcerated man, and never have to write me in jail or prison.

I want her to be surprised that her grandfather ever got arrested, ever went to jail. I want her to experience finding out that Grandpop did time with the same quizzical look she puts on her young face when she tastes strange food or can't figure out how to get the top off the marker. And I have the power to leave her that legacy by making different decisions than from my past.

My kids are grateful for the change, but they still have memories no child should have of their father. But I can leave them a new legacy by investing in myself and their families now that they are grown. We can talk honestly about things gone wrong and how to make things right. It's an opportunity some never get, and I am not wasting it.

A friend of mine always says that if he's having a bad day, he starts over, right then and there. He doesn't wait for tomorrow or a special occasion. There was a time when he would drown the sorrows of the day with Old Granddad in the mistaken belief that he could start over when he came to the next day. Only then he found out it didn't help, so he would repeat the cycle. Now, he has learned to start the day over, even if it's four in the afternoon. (And by the way, his grandchildren have never seen him drunk.)

I hope that older brother from Newark is getting to live out his new legacy. I hope you are as well. If not, you can start over right now.

Questions for Reflection:
1. What legacy do you want to leave your children or grand-children, and is a good legacy important to you? Why or why not?

2. Do you have an active and positive presence in your children's and grandchildren's lives? If not, why not?

3. As you reflect on your life, what good decisions do you need to make to leave a valued legacy to your children and grandchildren?

4. What changes must you be determined to make to leave your young loved ones your desired legacy?

5. Meditating on the need to make changes, what changes are included on your list?

6. Who do you need to enlist to help you to make these necessary changes?

7. How will you find supportive people to help you achieve your goal of a new legacy, for example, social workers, psychologists, mentors, and positive friends?

Do You Know That Someone Cried for You?

I saw it one day in a small church in Virginia. About a dozen people gathered for morning worship on a Sunday they will not soon forget. Everything seemed normal until the minister started preaching about life in prison. He talked about how many people in the Bible went to prison and how others, like David and Moses, would have caught murder charges in today's society.

The message was based on the familiar Bible verse, "I can do all things through Christ who strengthens me." No one there had thought about the fact that it was written from prison, an incarcerated man's declaration that his religious faith sustained him even in chains.

They heard the preacher talk about his journey through jail and his battle with alcoholism. They heard him and thought of their husbands: long bus rides away, phone calls that have to make do until the bid is over, the pain of separation. They came to the altar, and they cried.

They were crying for their husbands and their children. They were crying because it hurt to have them gone. They did not sign up for this; they did not fill out an inmate's application to be the wife, mother, or daughter. Their tears flowed from a mixture of emotion: the pain of separation, the reality of disappointment and betrayal, the frustration of life interrupted.

They held hands, cried, prayed, and promised to hold one another up in the journey. A dozen worshipers and nine of them made their way to that altar to pray and cry for their families and for us.

We can never undo our past. We can never reverse the mistakes in our rear view mirror, but we can live now in such a way that honors the tears, respects the emotions, and recognizes the sacrifices of those who missed us, those who waited for us, those who cried for us. We can live to witness against a system that makes it hard for them to stay in touch, flies their loved ones to remote states too expensive to visit, makes regular phone contact a financial luxury, and harasses visitors into thinking that they are serving time as well.

They cried over you that day because they know what you and your family went through and that so many don't care, having labeled the incarcerated as somehow less than human. But through their tears, they also recognized hope because they know that no human being is defined by their worst mistake. They know that there is some good in that husband, that son, that father. They know that while society will keep labeling a person as an ex-offender after the bid, they will have the opportunity to reject that label and see a human being with another chance. And tears of sorrow will become tears of joy.

Questions for Reflection:

1. Who is that one person in your life who you know cries and prays for you and will never give up on you? Ask that person what he or she sees in you that will not let that person give up on you.

2. Have you taken the time to think about what your loved ones went through when you were doing your bid? If so, what are your thoughts? If not, what do you think about it?

3. Think about the author's statement that even though your loved ones didn't sign up for this life of pain, disappointment, and betrayal, but they still love you, pray for you, and have hope for you. How does that make you feel? Have you cried for them?

4. As a result of your feelings regarding the above statement, what are you resolved to do in your life to make a positive change?

5. Does prayer have a place in your life? If so, what and whom do you pray for, and what are you asking to be done?

6. What can you now do that honors your tears and those of your loved ones and recognize the sacrifices of their missed moments of being with you?

7. Knowing your loved ones have hope for you and their hope and strength are in God, what hope do you have for yourself? In whom do you hope? What can you do to aid in realizing that hope?

How Is Your Health?

One of the more difficult things about making the transition back home is making sure you are staying healthy. It's not like the food you were eating in prison was healthy and organic, but at least it was somewhat balanced.

I had to go to the doctor my second week in jail because I had digestive problems. I told the doctor I was having gas problems (and that's not cool in closed quarters for you or your cellie) and sharp abdominal pains. He told me that everybody gets sick adjusting to the food. (If you know that, why not change it? Unless you don't want to spend money to ensure we eat right.) "Either you get constipated, or you get diarrhea," he said. "You'll eventually adjust." (I never did. I felt better when I ate out on work relief. Upon my release, I found a doctor who realized I had a gall bladder problem.)

At least I had access to some kind of medical care. Though often minimal and inconsistent, there was something. Now you're on your own. Once you get out, it's easy to avoid doctors altogether; eat what you want; and worse, stop taking meds.

There's no one to yell "Meds up" after you get home. And if you were on medication when you were gone, you need to see a doctor and check to see if you should continue. This goes for whether the treatment was for physical or mental health issues.

Check and see what benefits you may be entitled to under Medicare and Medicaid. There is a provision for health insurance for formerly incarcerated persons in the Affordable Care Act (http://www.pewtrusts.org/en/research-and-analysis/blogs/state-line/2013/04/05/exfelons-are-about-to-get-health-coverage). The Social Security office can help with that as well.

Find a reentry program that has resources to help you set up regular care for mental health, physical health, and dental work. (An unfounded belief among those incarcerated is that many prison dentists just pull teeth rather than provide extensive treatments.) Many churches and houses of worship have databases that can help, especially those trained in the Healing Communities Station of Hope model (http://www.healingcommunitiesusa.com/#!chapters/c1h8n). Prison Fellowship congregations do the same (https://www.prison-fellowship.org/resources/training-resources/reentry-ministry/on-going-ministry/helping-ex-prisoners-get-medical-care/).

But the real person responsible is you. Some of us just don't want to ask for help; others don't care. Some of us live in denial, and you know what DENIAL stands for: "Don't Even No I Am Lying."

In this book, we often discuss spending our time home making life better for others. But you can't do that if you're not healthy or, worse, have a health condition that makes you a further burden on others. You're worth it. Just ask the people who love you and waited for you. That's who sat with me while I recovered from gall bladder surgery.

Questions for Reflection:
   1. Think about whether your health is important to you? If yes, what are you doing to stay healthy? Or what are you doing to get healthy?

2. Are you taking your health for granted?

2. Are you taking anything for granted?

3. Are you employing a healthy perspective in your life?

4. Are you thinking negative thoughts before you fall asleep at night? If so, what are you doing to change those thoughts into positive ones?

5. Are you letting matters that are out of your control stress you out?

6. Are you putting enough effort into your relationships with loved ones, for example, spouse, significant other, parents, children, the divine presence?

7. Are you being true to yourself, or are you still in denial that all is well with you? If you are in denial, how do you plan to change? What will be your first step to positive change?

You Can't Change the Past, but You Don't Have to Live in It

That's why I never use the term *ex-offender*. That is, of course, unless I explain why I don't use the term *ex-offender*.

People should not have to wear a label describing their past as they move to the future. Bryan Stevenson of the Equal Justice Initiative often states, "No one should be defined by the worst mistake of their lives." That's exactly what we do when we refer to people as ex-offenders, ex-convicts, and ex-felons. The late Rev. Lonnie McLeod, who did 17 years in the New York state system before coming home and becoming a pastor, always said, "How would you like it if every time someone introduced you, they called you an ex-something?"

So I use the term *returning citizen*. Jondhi Harrell, founder of Philadelphia's Center for Returning Citizens, also uses that term. My colleague Glenn Martin, founding president of JustLeadershipUSA, uses *formerly incarcerated persons*, with the accent on *persons*. Others use *formerly justice involved*, or *have lived experience*. We are people, first and foremost, and that never changes, despite public efforts to label and dehumanize us.

I first heard the term *returning citizen* in Detroit in 2007. I attended a community and faith leaders meeting for people who had collectively rejected the term *ex-offender* and replaced it with *returning citizen*. We were developing a national strategy for helping churches, masjids, temples, and other houses of worship step up as reentry centers and decided this term we heard in Michigan should stick.

I took it on the road to Sacramento, California, in 2008 to a National Association for Prisoner Aftercare meeting led by my friend Joseph Williams. After using the term in a presentation, an elderly woman came up to me and asked, "Where'd you get that from?" I told her, "I was in Detroit–" And before I could finish, she hollered, "Praise the Lord! I knew it! I knew it!"

It turns out she was a retired school teacher who had provided GED instruction in the Michigan correctional system. When she left teaching, she wanted to help the men she knew were coming home. "I got in my prayer closet and asked the Lord for direction on how to help the ex-offenders. He told me, 'Don't call them ex-offenders; call them returning citizens.'" The term caught on with reentry agencies in the area, and now she was hearing it 2,000 miles away! Big things can come from small beginnings.

The District of Columbia passed legislation making *returning citizens* the official language of the city. College classrooms use the term. It's being used in Georgia's efforts in reforming reentry. President Obama used it in his executive order to "Ban the Box" for federal employment applications. The term isn't perfect, but it beats "ex-" labeling.

I refuse to be labeled as an ex-offender. My past will not define me. Once you get home, you can't let other people keep defining you by what you did. You can't change the past, but you don't have to live in it.

Questions for Reflection:

1. What do you believe the author is saying when he declares, "You can't change the past, but you don't have to live in it"?

2. Are you holding on to something that you need to let go of? In other words, are you living in your past?

3. What are you doing about what matters most in your life that will help you move on in the future?

4. What negative thoughts about yourself or your circumstance are keeping you from living in the past?

5. What first steps will you take to reverse your thinking to change your thoughts to positive corrective ones?

6. Whose help can you seek to help you in your efforts to look to your future with hope?

7. What do you most desire to accomplish in your life? What first steps will you take to achieve this aim?

Only a Punk Asks for Help

A strong man can deal with life on his own.

Strong women don't need nobody.

My life story is littered with evidence of those lies. Maybe yours is, too.

We often tell ourselves that we don't need help and that independence is a sign of strength until life shows up with situations that demand we seek help. Of course, we ignore it and believe the lie of self-sufficiency. And that makes our chances of making the transition from prison or jail back to the community all the more difficult.

My superman myth was interrupted recently by time in a mental health ward brought on by pure exhaustion and anxiety. Flat on my back, I thought about how my delusion of independence brought me to that room. My roommate got there the same way. We talked a lot about life after jail, hustling solo until it bit us in the behind.

We ended up in group therapy sessions, punks being told to "share our feelings" and "open up and talk about it." But before the sessions ended, we came to see the truth: All of us need someone to help along the way, someone to talk to, and share feelings. Doctors, teachers, addicts, construction workers, and drug dealers all in one room recognizing that feelings are part of life, and when you keep them bottled up inside, you end up acting up outside. A couple of guys showed up because their POs made them. They came in pissed off about being there but left recognizing that, despite the mistakes they made, they were human beings. Despite their reputation as heartless, they do have a heart. Despite their past, they still had a future. Some had anger management issues, but they discovered that they *could* control their tempers.

One brother said, "You know, sometimes I feel like a bomb ready to explode. My lady knows how to push my buttons. But when the police deal with a bomb, they defuse the bomb, not the detonator. I'm going to learn how to defuse the bomb in me, so that next time she hits the button—nuttin.'"

I listened, I talked, I even cried a few times, thinking about how ignoring my emotions had not made me strong but weak. The truth is that strong people ask for help because they are so strong that they don't give a (insert your term) what other people think about them when they do ask for help. It takes strength to ignore the people who think you're a punk because you got to take medication or go to a counselor, anger management classes, group therapy, rehab, detox, or family counseling.

"Ain't nothin' wrong with me." Keep telling yourself that stuff, and you'll believe the lie. There's something wrong with all of us, and the scars we carry, especially from being incarcerated, need healing. "Ain't nothin' wrong with me." Do you know what they call that in NA and AA? DENIAL, which stands for "Don't Even No I Am Lying."

Try saying it this way: "Ain't nothin' wrong with me that can't be fixed with some help from the right people, including myself." I had to learn that the hard way.

Questions for Reflection:

1. What lies or untruths about being a man are you believing?

2. In understanding that no one is an island and no one can do it all, how can you ask for help when you need it but not become dependent on the support of others when you don't?

3. Using ten words, describe yourself. Now write it in your journal. What is good about your notes in your description?

4. What lessons should you learn from erroneous thinking, such as "Ain't nothin' wrong with me"?

5. What were your five biggest mistakes? List them and think about them.

6. What lessons have you learned from each mistake? List them separately in your journal and how you will reverse your course.

7. When asking for help from someone, what questions should you ask yourself first? For instance, am I asking the right person for help? Why am I asking this person for help? Is there something I can do to help myself?

Chris Rock Offers Food for Thought

Chris Rock is funny. I can do without the vulgar language, especially the "N" word, but his humor opens up some serious stuff. Speaking of the "N" word, he talks in one bit about the difference between n***** and black people: He says that n***** want to be congratulated for things they are supposed to do. They will brag, "I ain't never been to jail," to which Rock replies, "You ain't supposed to go to jail! So what you want, a cookie?" They boast, "I take care of my kids." Rock's response is informative: "You supposed to take care of your kids, you low-expectation having [person]."

Yeah, I can do without the language, but not without the insight. A lot of us have low expectations of ourselves, and we are influenced by the low expectations others have of us. Some of them come from surprising places.

For instance, some come from the government. And I'm not talking about them building more jail cells because they expect that those of us who have been incarcerated are coming back. I'm not talking about building more prisons based on third-grade reading scores. I'm talking about reduced recidivism rates—high visibility, low expectations.

Many people talk today about reducing mass incarceration. Since 2010, the number of people in prison has gone down. Recidivism refers to how many come back for another bid, so reducing recidivism reduces incarceration rates since half of the released prisoners get arrested again. One third of all bids are for violations, not new crimes. So people want to see the recidivism rate reduced. They have pre-release and re-entry programs to help; they count the numbers. Recidivism is down, says the criminal justice system. We're successful, say the politicians.

"You low-expectation having [person]."

While not going back to jail or prison is good, it is a low expectation. The real issue is how well you are doing when you get home. How's your attitude? Are you making progress connecting or reconnecting with your kids? Are you building healthy relationships instead of playing people? How are you doing on your career plans or your education? Who is there helping you, supporting you, encouraging you in the process of becoming productive? Those are high goals to shoot for. Staying out is not enough. It's a minimal goal. It's a low expectation.

The jail I was in had a poor pre-release program. I often found myself working with guys on my block on their plans beyond the walls. When I asked them about their plans, they often said, "Well, the first thing is I ain't coming back here." Low expectation.

So we'll do an experiment. You can try it now. "Don't think of a fire truck." You know what you just did? Thought of a fire truck. Try it with somebody. It works, and it proves that anything you try to avoid becomes part of your consciousness. It rules you, holds you back.

You don't set a goal for what you don't want to do. That's low expectations. The challenge is to determine what you want to do, who you want to be. Aim for it, work for it, pray for it, and surround yourself with people who want it for you and work with you to get it. That's a high expectation...but you are worth it.

Every time someone tells me that recidivism rates are down, I nod and wonder how well guys are doing on the bricks. If you don't go back, you count as part of the reduction, even if you're homeless, living in a shelter, hate your baby mama, don't take care of your kids, can't find work, or sleeping on the street. You still count as a success for reduced recidivism. You deserve better.

Grab a high expectation beyond "I ain't going back." Let the politicians and corrections people pop the cork on reduced recidivism rates. You get champagne when you're reconciled with your family, have a new outlook on life, and make friends who have your best interest at heart and have your educational and career goals in view.

"Recidivism rates are down!"

"You low expectation having [person]."

Questions for Reflection:

1. How's your attitude? Are you caring for others as you care for yourself, or is it all about you?

2. Are you making progress connecting or reconnecting with your kids?

3. Are you building healthy relationships instead of playing people?

4. How are you doing on your career plans o your education? Do you dream and attempt to fulfill your dreams for yourself and your family?

5. Who is there helping you, supporting you, encouraging you in the process of becoming productive?

6. To what degree are you controlling the course of your life?

7. What worries you about your future, and how are you changing your worries into motivations to change your future?

Welcome Home 31

Success

Define it properly.

Surround yourself with others who know it and show it.

That's what I did on two days, in two states, listening to two different people speak on two topics, and with two things in common: success.

The first day, I listened to Darren Ferguson teach a class at New Brunswick Seminary. When I met him in 1996, he was wearing prison green, sweeping the floor of the chaplain's office at Sing Sing. He went from an 8½-to-20 bid for attempted murder in the second degree to deputy police chief of community affairs. He is also a pastor and a prisoner re-entry specialist. A loving family man, a good brother helps others. Success.

The second day, I listened to Glenn Martin. Glenn was there to build further the organization he had founded, JustLeadershipUSA, dedicated to reducing mass incarceration by 50 percent through training and developing leaders from those of us who have done time. Glenn pulled six years in the same New York correctional system as Darren. Since then, he has worked as a paralegal, a re-entry specialist, and a policy analyst, and now runs his consulting firm. He joys, more than at any time I hear him, over his young son, Joshua. Success.

Darren and Glenn will tell you that the keys to their success were opportunities and people. "Seeds," Martin called them, "which people planted into me." But he will tell you that he had to find the right people to do the planting. Ferguson talked about the church people who came to preach to the population while they were down but disappeared when he was about to come home. "All but one group," he says, "the white folks. They took me to their home, fed me at their table, and bought me my first suit. And when my wife died, they paid for the funeral. They are my family."

Other speakers at both events talked about how important it was to have someone invest in them, someone who believed in them, who didn't judge them by their resultant record from one mistake. Martin calls our country one of "lifetime punishment" because of what we go through when we get home. But he also knows that it can change if enough of us grab hold of our gifts and talents, surround ourselves with successful people, and then invest in others as well. Ferguson just uses one word: *More*. He says, "No matter who it is, I look at them and say, 'More.' There's more to you than people see and say, more to you than you or others give you credit for, more for God to do with you."

Those are guys I want to be around. Ferguson and I talk every week. I am a member of the organization Martin founded. They ooze success.

One last thing. I said you have to define success. I gave you some examples of work, family, and helping others. And when I have a tough time defining success, I start with, "It ain't what I was doing before, 'cause look where it landed me." They are out there. Successful people with jackets, on paper, refusing to be defined by their past and are committed to helping others change their future. Find one. Then be one.

Questions for Reflection:
   1. The author has provided you with two examples of success. How do you define success?

2. What does success look like in your life?

3. What do you value, and what is important to you?

4. What motivates and inspires you?

5. How do you react to the success of others? How do you respond to your accomplishments? Who do you attribute your actions—just yourself, or do you also thank those who helped you succeed?

6. What are your biggest strengths? What are your major weaknesses? What strategy have you developed to work to turn your weaknesses into strengths?

7. Who has a positive influence on you and will help you to succeed? If you have no one, how do you plan to seek, observe, and evaluate someone to be that valuable advisor?

Benjamin "Buck Benny" Mays

Buck and his father argued a lot before he left home. His father wanted him to work. Buck had other things in mind. That's why he left home at 16—other things. That's why he did what he did when he was almost 30: trespassing and theft of services.

Buck knew what he wanted and was not going to be stopped. You ever been there? You know what you want; Pops be damned. Buck wanted an education and to be a leader. Benjamin "Buck Benny" Mays was born in 1894 in Ninety-Six, South Carolina. That's not an address; that's the name of the town. His parents were born slaves. They sharecropped the land in an era of segregation. His school only opened four months a year so the kids could work as tenant farmers with their families. And that's where the fights with his father started.

His father wanted him to work the fields, but young Benjamin (he didn't get the name "Buck Benny" until he was in his 40s) wanted to go to school. Going four months a year from first grade took him ten years to finish elementary school. If it took you a long time to finish school, it probably wasn't because you worked on a farm.

Buck ran away from home at 16 but not to the streets. He ran away to enroll in seventh grade so he could finish high school. Did you leave home? Bet it wasn't to go *to* school.

But Buck wanted that education. He finished high school at 22 and went to college. He wanted to go to grad school so badly that he got his boys who worked on a train to get him a waiter's uniform. They were Pullman car porters who sneaked him onto the train (trespassing) where he pretended to be a waiter all the way to Chicago (theft of services). Then he got off the train and enrolled in the University of Chicago. I wonder how many charges a prosecutor would have hit him with to get him to plead down. When I broke into a place, it wasn't to go to school.

Ten years later, he was Dr. Mays. He went to Howard University and became a dean, then he became president of Morehouse College. In 1944, he lowered the age for admission to the college to get younger students in who wouldn't be drafted so he could keep the school open. He let in a 15-year-old who hadn't finished high school. You might have heard of him: Martin Luther King Jr. Mays found ways to get money to keep the school open. That's why they called him "Buck Benny." How'd you get your handle?

Mays advised King through the Civil Rights Movement, advised presidents Kennedy, Johnson, and Carter and gave the eulogy at King's funeral. Dr. Mays became president of the Atlanta School Board and wrote nine books. He wanted it.

Running away from home, Mays finished elementary school at 16, high school at 22. He broke the law to go to school, not stay out of it, and he changed the world.

You have a whole life ahead of you, no matter how hard the first part has been—problems at home, run the streets, participation in an "alternative economy." But you can write the rest of the story, and it can be positive if you want it badly enough. Ask Martin Luther King how a runaway changed his life.

Questions for Reflection:

1. Is there someone in your life who has inspired you to change for the better?

2. What characteristics and traits about this person encourage you to be someone who leaves a positive mark in your family, on your community, in your city?

3. What struggles has this person overcome that impressed you?

4. What lasting positive effect has this person had on your life?

5. How do you plan to share what you have learned from this person with others?

6. As a result of the positive effect this person had on your life, what do you desire to pass on to others so that they can light someone else's way?

7. What does the life of Benjamin Mays tell you about the importance of determination and commitment?

Graduation (Education)

I always look forward to graduation because it's not just finishing; it's a start. That's why they call it "commencement exercises." I knew I wanted to get a PhD when I first graduated from Morehouse College 50 years ago. When I saw all those black professors with robes from Harvard, Yale, and Columbia, I said to myself, "Gots to get me one of those!"

But my favorite graduations were at Sing Sing prison in upstate New York. I was the dean for the masters programs at New York Theological Seminary, so I had to go to sign diplomas and shake hands. The guys spoke. They had just finished 42 credits in ten months, so they were like co-valedictorians. Some of them are still there. Twenty years later, some have died. Some of them I still see sometimes as they're home now. They're pastors, social workers, teachers, running agencies, or serving as consultants. But when I saw them each of those six years at graduation, something went through me. They were proud of what they had accomplished, and they were about to start getting busy in prison jobs such as teachers, chaplain's assistants, and social workers.

Getting an education while locked up is one of the best ways to come home and stay home. And while many states cut back funding for college classes in prison, schools are finding ways to get inside. The recent Second Chance Pell Grant legislation has made federal funds available for college in prison. You may not be ready for college yet, but don't tell me you're not college material. Every guy I taught at Sing Sing had a felony conviction, and some had bodies. Some had to learn to read and then get their GED while locked up.

My guys at Sing Sing and Holmesburg, Green Haven, Curran-Fromhold, DC Jail, and the Alexandria Detention Center are some of the best students. They always read the books, wrote the papers, and finished the assignments. You are capable of being in that number. You can do this.

So I will put on my blue and green robe this weekend and march in commencement. It's not as cool as Sing Sing graduations, but I have students whose fathers are doing bids at my current school, plenty of grads over the years as well. And those are just the ones whose stories I know. But I'll be thinking of Sing Sing. And, hey, "you gots to get you one of those!"

Questions for Reflection:
1. Are you using your time wisely? If so, what are you doing to further yourself toward your goals? If not, why not?

2. What makes you nervous or uncomfortable when you think about getting a college degree?

3. When did you last push the boundaries of your comfort zone concerning achieving a college degree or a trade certification?

4. Which is worse: failing or never trying to achieve something? Explain your answer in your journal.

5. Affirmations are positive statements that can help you to challenge and overcome self-sabotaging and negative thoughts. An example of one is: I look forward to the future and my role in helping others in it! Now write at least three affirmations, one for your physical health, career aspiration, and mental health.

6. Do you know in which career field you envision working? Why? How do you plan to positively impact the lives of others through your chosen career path?

7. What is stopping you from getting started? Who can you elicit to help you get started?

You're the One Who Missed It!

Those words came stinging back to me that day. I was looking at a picture of graduates of my school, Howard University, splashed across the front page of *The New York Times*. They were part of the audience for President Obama's commencement address at "HU—U KNOW!"

I knew one of the students in the picture. That student has a father doing a bid. I met Moms, Grandma, and Auntie at the reception, but Pops couldn't be there. He was unavoidably (heck, maybe avoidably) detained.

I know what it's like to miss it. I missed my daughter's twenty-first birthday. We did talk on the phone, though, and I went back to my part of the block, looking sideways so no one would see the tears form. "You missed it," said the voice in my brain, working its familiar guilt trip formula on my feelings. "But at least I called her. She knows I care," roared back the daddy in me that refused to allow bars and wire to separate me from that little girl who was growing into a marvelous lady.

I thought about that when I saw my student in that picture. I wondered what else her Pops had missed. Meeting her first boyfriend? prom night? high school graduation? college?

When I came home, I said I wasn't going to miss nothing.

Then it happened. Better put, *I* happened. Family gathering, everybody was there but me. There was no self-care plan, a relapse, and no responsibility. "Can't let them see me like this." And I missed it again.

When I called her to apologize, my daughter was forever gracious. She accepted my apology, but she ain't a little girl anymore, so she stood up to her Pops and said, "Daddy, you're the one who missed it!"

She had told me she wished I was there, but she wasn't going to run a guilt trip on me. She's too smart for that. She simply pointed out that while we as fathers are often the bad guy because we miss special events like birthdays, proms, weddings, and graduations, our kids make it anyway. Many of them use our absence as motivation to do better.

But my daughter pointed out something we don't talk about. When we miss an event because of incarceration or intoxication, in jail or indifference, mama drama or money's funny, we lose a part of ourselves because *we* missed it. I should have been there not just for her, but for me because my kids and grandkids are part of me, and to miss their events is to miss part of my own soul. I owe it to myself to be part of their lives.

Sometimes we are avoidably detained by fears or faults, addictions or attitudes. Not gonna let that happen again now that I'm home. After all, one day, she might be on the cover of *The New York Times*.

Questions for Reflection:

1. List your top five greatest mistakes that caused you to miss special events in your children's, parents', or significant others' lives? Now write down the circumstances surrounding you being missing in action from your loved ones' lives.

2. Why is it important to look back at what happened, analyze it, and assess what changes need to be made to change your behavior and attitude?

3. Why is it important to accept responsibility for missing the event or celebration?

4. Think about how you can create new special events to share with your loved ones. Realizing that you are not trying to make up for what happened in the past, you are creating new special memories!

5. List all the special people for whom you need to create special memories to share.

6. List at least five unique events you can create to share with those special in your life as a way of creating new positive memories.

7. What special memory of you do you want your loved ones to recall when you are gone?

Sound Decision-Making Keeps You Out and From Regret

I remember when I still had another year to walk off my probation. In April 2017, I got off the paper and got out of the system for the first time in ten years! But a year before that, I was thinking.

The truth is, I don't often think about it now. But it weighed on me then. Even though I still reported to probation once a month, that last year I did it online. (In fact, I almost forgot one day because it was my birthday.) But I only had to sit in my PO's office twice a year. The rest is answering questions from my "Virtual PO." Do you know why it became that light for me that last year?

Risk factor.

They are coming up with new ways to assess whether we will probably re-offend, whether we will offend while waiting for trial, or whether we'll offend upon release. It's all about risk factors. They factor in employment status, family support, and a whole lot of stuff. But one thing they are trying to measure now is called "impulsivity." Impulsivity. Risk factor. It can mess with your case.

Impulsivity is simply the failure or ability to think through a decision and its consequences before you take action. If you just react, you have high impulsivity. High impulsivity equals higher risk. They know you don't think through your decisions and do whatever feels right rather than considering other ways of dealing with reality. And your case hangs on it.

Still not feeling me?

A friend of mine went upstate to a prison to visit a young man. This was a special supervised visit because the dude he was visiting shot and killed his son. My man was going to prison to forgive his son's killer, 12 years after the fact. When they met, trigger man blurted out, "I'm sorry for what I did, man. When I shot your son, I wasn't thinking about what might happen to me, and I damn sure wasn't thinking about what could happen to your family or mine. I'm sorry."

Impulsivity.

Now dude had 12 years to think about it and wished he hadn't pulled that trigger. But the time he should have thought about it was before he shot. That's high impulsivity.

I don't know what you did your bid for, but it was probably an impulsive act, and you didn't think about all the consequences to you or your family and friends. But that's one of the things they are looking at for sentencing, release, and forms of probation and parole. And real rap, we need to deal with our impulsivity not just for the state's sake, but for our own. When we develop the ability to think things through before we act, we develop a measure of control over our lives that helps make them more manageable, more under control.

I know a guy who came home after ten years. His brother was dead, and so he became the second father to his niece. One day, the niece's boyfriend beat her. My man had an impulse to take dude out, but then he stopped and thought it through. "If I whack this dude, I go back to prison, and my niece ain't got me home no more." So he and his niece went to the station and turned dude in. Then he used his energy to organize a march against domestic violence and violence against women, raising money for the cause. He had done something about what happened to his niece, and he was still home to take care of her. He thought it through to its logical outcome and made a better decision.

If you have a problem with decision-making, you can't control your impulsivity, get help. See a counselor, a pastor, an imam, or someone you can talk to about your decision-making. Thinking it through can make the difference between staying home and another bid. Showing you know how to do it gives the state something to work with when determining your risk factor. And you will have peace of mind to know that you're a real man or woman because you got stuff under control.

Questions for Reflection:
1. Given the author's definition for *risk factor* and your assessment of your current state of existence, how would you rate your risk factor, high or low, and why?

2. List at least three examples of what you have done that would cause your risk factor to be high? How can you change your reasoning process to lower your risk factor of returning?

3. Given the author's definition for *impulsivity* and your evaluation of your current decision-making process, how would you rate your impulsivity, high or low, and why?

4. List at least three instances of your thought process that would cause your impulsivity to be considered high, causing you to react instead of thinking through the logical and most beneficial way of responding for all concerned?

5. What do you value most in life? Why? What is most important to you in life?

6. What do you believe? What principles do you cherish?

7. Ponder your tendencies to react to certain situations? Are your reactions negative or positive? What are you thinking? Self-examine what you need to do differently to change for the good of yourself and others.

Welcome Home 36

Nobody Would Listen to Me

It was my second week on the block. Tuesday, around 10:00 PM was meds call. I stood in line for my medications, and when I reached the front, I had a question for the nurse. I don't remember what I asked, but I remember his frustrated response: He shut down med call and retreated to the exit. The CO screamed at me, "See what you did!" I formed my mouth to say that I only asked the nurse a question, but I didn't have time. The CO was screaming unintelligibly in my ear, chasing me back to my bunk, where I flopped. And for the first time in that jail, I cried.

Everybody does, at least one night. And the tears all flow from the same source: a fundamental recognition that your life seemingly doesn't count, the world goes on without you, nobody will hear you, and nobody will listen to you.

Ongoing prisoner strikes in several states reminded me of how nobody listens to incarcerated men, women, and children. No one hears them complain about lack of programming, over-crowded conditions, or dehumanizing behavior. No one listens because our culture still points fingers, hellbent on repeating, "If you can't do the time, don't do the crime," trapped in its own world where justice equals revenge. No one listens.

But they were beginning to listen when residents of cor-rectional facilities in Alabama, Michigan, and Florida were documented as holding work stoppages on September 9, 2016, the forty-fifth anniversary of the protests at the Attica, New York state prison facility. In Alabama, even the COs stayed out for a shift. They knew that the same overcrowding that threatened inmate safety affected them as well.

More protests have come and gone, but few listen when people complain about work conditions and compensation in prison. Netflix documentary *13th* surprised many by revealing that the constitutional amendment of that number abolishes slavery for all but the incarcerated. So labor performed for ten cents an hour or a dollar a day is perfectly legal in the United States, and in states like Alabama and Texas, they are not paid at all! Now the "slaves" are on strike. Texas and South Carolina prison officials denied it had come their way, but accounts received by the Marshall Project stated otherwise.

Few new outlets reported it. They are tied to the corporate entities that benefit from the enslaved labor of prisoners. From workers' uniforms to women's undergarments, to the food that reaches American tables from recognized groceries to the 10,000 beef cattle, 20,000 pigs, and 250,000 egg-producing chickens tended by the agribusiness division of the Texas Department of Corrections (where no one gets paid and refusal to work means solitary confinement). But as long as oil companies use prison labor to do toxic oil cleanup and incarcerated people to replace "costly" unionized operators, it's a stretch to think that news outlets dependent on their advertising dollars will listen and report fairly.

No one listens, and then strikes happen, and people begin to take notice. No one listens when you come home either, not to you because you don't exist anymore, replaced by a label— *ex-felon*, *ex-offender*, *ex-con*. Your voice is stilled by a society that refuses to recognize your humanity.

But something stirs within you because deep within, you know you the person exists, and you have a voice. If a formerly incarcerated person speaks in a forest, and there is no one around to hear them, do they make a sound? Yes, you do, because no one can deny that the Creator creates and knows, as do you, that you are alive with a purpose and, hopefully, a plan to make them hear you.

That's why I write the way I do. That's why I teach the way I do at the university. That's why I preach the way I do in the pulpit. That's why I will be at the front of the line on election day. If you can't vote, make sure everybody you know who can does vote. I have a voice, and I refuse to let this society's labels of *ex-prisoner*, *drunk*, or anything else define me. That's why I support organizations like JustLeadership USA and Community Connections for Youth, and those people inside the system and outside the walls who work for change and a society that recognizes the worth of all human beings.

It's why I try to feel some sympathy for the screaming CO. Because nobody listens to him either. I didn't. We listened to his uniform and his badge, not him. He has no voice either; he's a cog in a wheel. I have to pray for him just to keep me from smugly thinking, *He and I are the same, except I have a good education, and he has a BS job*. Yeah, I need prayer, too.

Questions for Reflection:

1. Do you feel people are not listening to you? My mother said, "If you want people to listen to you, spend time listening to them." In other words, once we begin to empathize or put ourselves in others' situations, they begin to take time to do the same for us. What are your thoughts?

2. Have you ever heard that it is vital to engage people, connect with people, and serve people, then they will listen to

you? This simply means find topics that interest both and then engage people and share your thoughts. It helps us to broaden our interests and to appreciate our differences. Is this something you are willing to try to do? If you have studied the subject, you can offer your assistance in making change occur, as the work stoppages in the prison facilities discussed in this piece. Thus, you will have engage, connect, and serve!

3. Sometimes when we get overly self-absorbed with ourselves and what we want, others see it as selfishness, which can hinder others from listening to us. When have you been overly preoccupied with you and caused others to lose their opportunity to get what they needed, such as the author's situation in asking a question instead of accepting his meds?

4. What have you done lately to get people to listen to you?

5. What questions or struggles do you still have in getting people to listen to you? Listen to them, and then share with someone you trust, and you know it will help you.

6. What do you need to change about yourself to get people to listen to you?

7. What is your Creator calling you to do to help yourself and others, thereby improving your relationship with others?

I'm Still Here

That's a line often used by a certain TV preacher that gets a lot of play. He tells his congregation, "Look at your neighbor in the eye and tell them, 'I'm still here!' Despite all I've been through, 'I'm still here!'"

You have a right to say that today. You don't need to turn to a neighbor. You can look in a mirror (or whatever they hang above the sink if you're still in a bid) and tell yourself, "I'm still here!"

There are people you know who are dead and gone. "I'm still here!"

You know someone doing life without parole. "I'm still here!"

You've been arrested, thrown in the squad car, stuffed into a holding cell, eaten stale baloney sandwiches, endured a nasty cell, been faced down by COs, plea-bargained by the process. "I'm still here!" Damn that process. Malcolm Feeley wrote a book called *The Process Is the Punishment*. He ain't never lied. It is. But "I'm still here!"

Nicole Gonzalez Van Cleve's book *Crook County* talks about how racist and dehumanizing Chicago's Cook County jail system is, from degrading defendants (they call them "mopes") to flexing on families. Pages upon pages of eyewitness accounts of everything from prosecutors laughing at perps' language skills to sheriff's violently threatening our moms in the courtroom. I've been through it; you've been through it. "I'm still here!"

Sentenced, warehoused, the SHU, no programs, assaults, face downs, stand-downs, lockdowns, no visits. "I'm still here!"

No parole, lame pre-release programs, reentry trauma, PO tension, "I'm still here!"

Trying to fit in with the family, baby mama drama, baby daddy drama, revenge, remorse, rejection. "I'm still here!"

Job issues, school problems, can't vote, can't live here, but "I'm still here!"

Nobody wants to give you a second chance, let alone a seventh or seventy times seven chance. "I'm still here!"

I spoke to a group of female inmates in the Iowa Correctional Facility for Women in 2014. I told them, "I wasn't arrested; I was rescued!" The place erupted with amens and applause. I asked the pastor who invited me why that happened. She said, "Most of the women I talk to here tell me, 'If I wasn't arrested when I was, I'd probably be dead by now.'" They got it. "I'm still here!"

So you are still here. So what? First, be grateful. Most people ask, "Why me?" when the stuff hits the fan. How about asking, "Why me?" when you recognize that as bad as stuff may get, "I'm still here!"

Second, look around. There's more to life than your stuff. There is a world with people who can benefit from your story and get hope from you still being here. I often get pissed about getting clean and sober so late in life until I realize that in my story there is hope for a senior citizen (okay, an old head) to get clean after 50, 60—heck, maybe 70! There are no hopeless people, only people without hope. I read somewhere that sobriety brings the promise that "no matter how far down the scale we have fallen, we will discover that our experience can benefit others."[1] Hey, my enzymes are off, my brain cells ain't all there, but "I'm still here."

You're still here because you ain't through. You ain't done. You have purpose. There's a reason you ain't six feet under. You got stories to tell, people to help, children to raise, young people who need to see evidence of change, hundreds of "Crook County" systems to change, work projects that need to be done, and a life that needs to be lived. It may be your second chance, a third chance, fiftieth chance, or last chance. But despite all the stuff that has happened, no matter the pain or the wound—even self-inflicted—grab gratitude for learning from your past and keep your head up for the future. Tell yourself and the world, "I'm still here!"

Questions for Reflection:

1. What does the phrase *I'm still here!* mean to you and your criminal justice experience?

2. What does the phrase *I'm still here!* bring to your mind when you think about poor decisions made that may have been the cause of your incarceration?

3. Having survived your criminal justice experience, what three traits helped you to survive and be able to state today, "I'm still here!"?

4. What encouragement did someone offer you that helped you to keep surviving?

5. List the people who helped you keep your sanity while going through your struggles with incarceration and nightmares following your ordeal.

6. Do you have a gratitude page in your journal for each day you arise, think, breathe, and have soundness of mind? Why do you believe the author thinks it is vital to "grab gratitude" for learning from your past?

7. The author advises you to "keep your head up for the future." My father told me, "When you keep your head up, no one can ride your back." Ponder this statement, and write an affirmation to help you live it.

[1]*Alcoholics Anonymous*; page 83.

That Was the Scariest [Stuff] I Ever Done"

His hands were shaking as he thought about what he had just done. These were ordinarily steady hands that knew how to grip a knife. These were hands that never shook when they held a gun. But they shook now.

"That was the scariest [stuff] I ever done."

Scary. His face had looked danger in the eye. He needed no street credit check. But this was scary. Looking into the face of the mother of the child he had assaulted was terrifying. But he knew it was time to man up and take responsibility for what he had done. Say "I'm sorry." Show remorse. Scary [stuff].

The boy's mother had said of him, "I hate his guts for what he did. If he were standing in front of me, I would have no trouble getting my machete (not "*a* machete," but "*my* machete"), hacking him to pieces, burying them under my cellar, and sleeping that night peacefully for the first time since he attacked my son."

But in the same breath, that mother wanted peace on the streets. Knowing that the young man whose hands would shake had a three-year bid, knowing he would be back on the streets sooner rather than later, she chose to agree to have him put in a program, Common Justice, where he had the potential to change. She wanted him to man up, take responsibility, become a contributor to society, and drop the menace label.

Scary [stuff]. Manning up. Scary.

At some point, we all have to do it. Whatever we have done to get us in the system, whether it was a crime we committed or just being in the wrong place at the wrong time, at some point, we have to man up, woman up, grow up, and accept responsibility. It's scary. It means looking at our actions, yes, but also the attitudes behind the actions. That's what my man had to do to get to the place where he made his scary admission. He had to say, "I'm sorry for what I did."

In the documentary *The Interrupters*, outreach worker Cobe Williams takes a young man who gets out of jail to visit the barbershop he robbed. He announces his apology to the barbers, to the patrons, to mothers who had young children with them who sat terrified in that same shop the day he and his boys burst in guns drawn. There were plenty of tears to go around that day, but it had to be done. Dude had to man up and sincerely mean it when he said he was sorry. Scary. Later in the movie, he gets a job as a janitor for a daycare center. He went from terrorizing kids to making life better for them.

Looking within ourselves is scary, especially when we know we'll find something we don't like, especially when we will be confronted with the violence that has been done against us, leaving us hurt and bitter and ready to inflict pain on others. Sometimes we have bought into the notion that we are serial menaces, animals with no regard for others. But an honest review of the past reveals that we have been victims, far more so than many others. Yes, we have done things that got us in the system, but something had been done to us that hurt us first, and the unresolved pain turned on us. Hurt people hurt people. We were, and we did.

So dude with the shaky hands got help. He got into a program that would help him heal from his pain. He got with people who would understand his inner turmoil and turn it inside out. He needed to know that the true feelings didn't make him a punk, but that dealing with them would make him a man.

Change is scary, but he found a place and people who could look at his shaking hand and not reject him, listen to his trembling voice and not mock him, watch his eyes well up with tears and not call him soft. Nobody who's soft could face his victim's mom as he did. In that scary place, he found he could be part of that mother's healing. When he gets through this scary [stuff], she won't need a machete, and the system won't need a bed for him. He manned up and grew up, and his change will be an investment in the change in his community.

Questions for Reflection:
   1. What is your scary [stuff]?

   2. What does it mean for you to man up or woman up as the author suggests?

   3. What negative behaviors, traits, and characteristics do you need to remove?

4. Are there people who are not suitable for you to associate with or be around? If so, why? If not, what happened causing your incarceration? What do you need to change or drop to live a more productive life?

5. Are there people to whom you need to make amends to move on with your life?

6. Are there people you need to release or forgive so that you can move on with your life?

7. Your subconscious mind is where your self-image is stored. All of your attitudes, experiences, beliefs, and values are stored deep in your subconscious, driving your behavior and forming the core of who you are. Understanding this, here is a visual exercise for you to do. Create a box, a vision board, or some other medium to store and display who you are and what your hopes and dreams are for the future.

Just Made Me a Dolphin

I looked at my friend. I think she recognized the confusion on my face. I am usually up on terms, but I missed *dolphin*.

"They shot my nephew in the head, you know, a hole in the head, like a dolphin." All I could do was sigh. I felt bad for my friend and whispered a silent prayer. My head jolted when she said, "I'm praying for the guy who shot my nephew."

Her pastor was even more shocked than I was. He knew she worked with people in prison and jails and their families. We both knew that she had written letters to persons convicted of crimes violent and nonviolent, encouraging them as they did their time. She had organized a group of church ladies to assist her in work, a team of women visiting, writing, and advocating for people behind bars. But praying for the dude who shot your nephew, your family member?

"Yes," she told her pastor. "All these young men need us. It could have been the other way around; my nephew could have shot him. I love my nephew, but if the guy who shot him needs us from the church, we're there!" She meant it. I thought about the gospel song "Somebody Prayed for Me." Who knows how many people prayed for me when I was locked up. Who knows how many people who prayed for you and are still praying for you.

So she is praying on both sides: healing for her nephew and restoration for his shooter. But is it really two sides? Aren't we in this together, one community, one cause? My friend could pray for both sides because she only saw one side—two young men who needed help and healing, spiritual and physical. If there are two sides, it's two sides of the same coin, and we need to focus on the coin.

"Young people know revenge and violence because we live in a violent world and a violent country. They pick up the culture because they don't see anything else," offers Will Latif Little, a Philadelphia barber who did ten years for third-degree murder before turning things around and providing mentoring programs for local youth. "A lot of them don't want to hurt people, but there's peer pressure and all kinds of expectations on them from the culture." Will's story of redemption will appear in full next week. But I needed him to tell me how to deal with forgiveness and not appear to be a punk, not be soft.

"We can show them how our lives have changed," he said, "and as guys who've been on the streets, we have credibility." I thought about Credible Messengers, the DC antiviolence initiative that turns the voices of older men toward the lives of younger men and adolescents with words designed to stop the violence, heal the divisions, interrupt the conflicts, and show new ways to build the community. It is happening, and around the country, people are saying, "It ain't got to be this way. I ain't got to be this way!"

The National Institute of Justice published a paper exploring the causes for the rise in recent homicide rates. The author, Richard Rosenfeld, a professor from the University of Missouri-St. Louis, considers three popular explanations: rise in heroin markets, more people coming home from jail and prison, and general animosity toward law enforcement made worse by recent police brutality (they call it the Ferguson Effect). Any way you slice it, all three explanations blame you and your community, you out there slinging heroin for white kids, you shouldn't have been let out of prison, you got a chip on your shoulder that says, "Forget law enforcement, to hell with laws." No one's willing to look at an unjust system, racial bias, and economic hardship. But at the end of the day, with all the madness around you, you can still decide your path. My friend chose prayer over revenge, seeing that the two sides of the dispute are two sides of the same coin, and she's about saving the coin and making things right.

The next chapter is a full interview with Will Latif Little, Charles Hodges, and Qadir on how they made the shift from violence to peace, from the desolate to the resolute. And in it, there's a glimpse of answers to my friend's prayers.

Questions for Reflection:
1. What resentment or hurt are you harboring that you need to forgive?

2. Understanding that forgiveness is about extending mercy to those who've harmed us, even if they don't deserve it,[1] why is it important to forgive others?

3. One way to build a forgiving heart is to commit to doing no harm, as did the woman who prayed for the young man who shot her nephew in the head. Instead of harboring revenge or hatred, she prayed for the young man to soften his heart through divine intervention. Are you ready to pray for those who have hurt you or have offended you?

4. Another way to practice forgiveness is to put yourself in the other person's shoes, or simply put, attempting to understand or empathize with the other person's position or what caused him or her to commit such an act. Have you tried to understand or empathize with the person or persons who have caused you pain?

5. Understanding that unforgiveness can harm you internally (your body) or, worse, cause you to lash out and do another bid, isn't it time to meditate on ways to forgive and pray for yourself, asking for the strength to forgive?

6. Consider ways you can attend to your inner pain. The best way is to figure out who hurt you and why? Now, list the persons that come to mind and make sure you spend quiet time uncovering the why.

7. One way to discover the who's and the whys is to look at the people closest to you in your youth, family members, early school experiences, and others. Attempt to uncover how your suffering has helped your growth and hindered your formation of lasting positive relationships. Are you ready to start the process of forgiveness? In what ways can you use your success through your approach to help others?

---

[1] *8 Keys to Forgiveness (8 Keys to Mental Health)*, by Robert Enright (W. W. Norton & Company, 2015).

It Was Eatin' Me Alive!

Qadir thought back on those days, the days when he knew that the man who had shot and killed his brother had been released from prison.

"It was eatin' me alive!"

Qadir had been on the move and not just physically stalking his brother's killer. He also moved back and forth about what he should do. The streets demanded revenge, but his heart moved back and forth between the solutions of revenge and forgiveness. That journey was the one that caused frazzled nerves, medication, and mental anguish.

His childhood friend, Chuck Hodges, had held up a sign pointing to forgiveness. "The brother has changed," he said, speaking of the man whose trigger finger now tapped out lessons on the computer for young boys and adults with advice for getting out of the game and living a purposeful life. That same game held up a sign, "You know what you should do. An eye for an eye." Challenging journey, hard choice, two directions.

On that journey, Qadir wondered what other people on the street would think of him for forgiving the man. Having done a bid himself, he also factored in what would happen if he followed the code of the streets. "He'd lose his life, and I'd have lost my life, back to the penitentiary." In the end, after years on a journey that was eating him alive, Qadir strode into the barbershop where his friend, Charles, worked. Working two chairs away was the man who shot his brother. Qadir grabbed him, held him, and forgave Will "Latif" Little for the killing that had happened almost two decades ago. Their story is told in the documentary *Behind the Bullet*.

Qadir's journey is not unique, the trip between the two signs, that is. If you are honest, you know there is a tug-of-war between the revenge of the streets and trying to make a new start, being a bigger, better person. But too often, the streets win. A lot of that, says Will, is that "many youths don't see examples of living a different way." They know deep down that the game is harmful to themselves, their families, and the community, but the examples of alternatives are few.

And the cost, says life coach Iyabo Onipede, a returning citizen who began reaching out to others while still on paper, is challenging the old signs that point to the streets and the streets themselves where you learned to be who you are. "All of us know that our life experiences help us build the person we become. The person we become is tied to our experience, like a tetherball to a pole. Change often means cutting some ties, not just to your past, but the way your past shapes your present." Charles Hodge held up a sign for Qadir. "You're better than that! It ain't got to be that way!" It's the same sign that Will holds up for the young men in his mentoring program. And now, all three of them hold that sign together as part of a new initiative: Team Redemption, Forgiveness, and Peace.

Together, Will, Qadir, and Charles speak at schools, prisons, jails, mentoring programs, churches, and peace rallies offering alternatives to violence and retaliation. They have shown their vision of change to students at Job Corps and on the radio. Qadir points to the man who killed his brother and says, "Today, I love this brother!" Charles represents the group with his clothing brand, Team RFP. Will preaches focus to young people in the high school where he was once expelled.

Forgiveness may seem like a punk thing to do. But deep down, we all want it. We were constructed for redemption, created for peace, and crafted to forgive and be forgiven. It's in you. And with Qadir, Charles, and Will, as well as others, you have a sign.

Questions for Reflection:

1. When we experience unforgiveness, hatred, and anger, it affects our bodies, thinking, and behavior. Our heart rate increases, breathing more rapidly, muscles tense, blood flow is redirected to them, and our liver releases glucose. Are you experiencing any of these symptoms? Or are you experiencing mental anguish? If so, what are you doing about it?

2. The author talks about Qadir's inner thinking. Are you experiencing similar thoughts? Do you understand how this internal battle is affecting your health emotionally, mentally, and physically? What toll is it affecting on your well-being? Is it worth it to think of positive alternatives to unforgiveness and the negative feeling you are experiencing?

3. Your body prepares for battle, and you experience headaches, insomnia, high anxiety, high blood pressure, and are an increased risk for a stroke! Is all this worth holding on to your unforgiveness? Not to mention that if you act out your scheme for retaliation, you will possibly take a life and lose your freedom (life) in the process.

4. Isn't it time to forgive if for no other reason to save your life? What positive steps will you take to forgive?

5. Are you willing to join an organization such as Qadir to help you with the process of forgiveness and with helping others?

6. Are you willing to reach out for help? If so, what organizations or individuals will you seek to help you in this journey?

7. In addition to Qadir's method, you can seek help from a doctor, psychologist, pastor and build up a positive support system of family, friends, among others. Are you ready to get started? Write an affirmation with your ultimate goal in mind and write it down ten times a daily and recite it at least ten times a day.

Chaos Is Cash

How many people did you feed today? Or, better put, how many people did you feed when you were locked up?

I know I fed quite a few. The DOC employees made their money, including overtime, because I messed around and got myself locked up. And every time one of us screwed things up, they got more work. No wonder that a dude I know who works in corrections told me, "Our COs don't like you volunteers. Y'all trying to bring some order and life in this place, but some of those COs got a saying: 'Chaos is cash!'"

I fed some stockholders, too. I was in a facility run by a for-profit company that made money on my misery. A lot of for-profit prison companies get paid by the bed per their contract, so it is in their best interest to keep the place full, cut corners on services, and maximize profits for their owners, executives, and shareholders.

Simply stated, these for-profit companies ensure that their facilities are full through their contractual agreements with jurisdiction because the jurisdiction must pay the penalty if they fall below the required number of residents. You read about the one company that understaffed their prison in Idaho to save money while having staff file false time sheets so they could be seen "in compliance" with corrections regulations. They had more assaults there than in the other state prisons combined. Chaos is cash.

Food companies made money off me. Commissaries charge for food you know you have to have to offset whatever is institutional fare. Today, there are food companies that I won't buy from because they got my money when I was locked up. Oh, except for those noodles. I stopped eating them while I was in jail. You ain't making me no noodles without washing your hands first, yo. I spoke at an event when I got out, and the people gave me a fruit basket as a gift with a bag of those noodles in it as a joke. It was in a church, so I had to edit my response.

Pre-selected food vendors are making money off of inmates and their families because families can no longer send loving care packages to their loved one but must use these vendors. Chaos is Cash! And some companies make money off of cheap jail and prison labor, 20 cents an hour for work that should pay 75 times the amount! That's slavery, which by the way, is still legal in the United States if you are in prison or jail. Check the thirteenth amendment that ended slavery. There's an exception for convicts.

So why tell you all this stuff today? First, because it's wrong for people to make so much money from the incarceration complex. That's misery money and creates the incentive to lock up people to make money off them. But it's also an incentive for me to live in a way where I am not forced to feed someone else's kids. I got enough trouble feeding my own.

I used to work with a teacher who told students, "Keep acting up. You're gonna make sure some country boy has a job upstate." Well, here's a newsflash, country boy: The system has pitted us against each other because it doesn't like you either. You didn't grow up wanting to be a CO, but the system took over the farm business, closed the steel mill, and moved industry for profit's sake, and now you are stuck in a job you don't want either. It ain't you versus us; it's the two of us versus something bigger. And you're feeding their kids, too.

Questions for Reflections:

1. From what you have read in this piece, what does "Chaos is cash" mean to you?

2. Are you prepared to help galvanize your community to change for-profit vendors so that people are not disadvantaged or mistreated for others' profit.

3. Are you willing to become involved as a reform advocate working to right wrongs, such as for-profit prison companies getting paid to keep their facilities full because such practices encourage these companies to cut corners on services to inmates while maximizing profits for their owners, executives, and shareholders?

4. The author requests that you "check the thirteenth amendment that ended slavery." Does this motivate you to stop any practices that allow inmates' labor to be exploited in the United States?

5. The author states that such practices are "misery money." How is it misery money? How did such practices affect you during your bid?

6. If you were not negatively impacted, recall and write down what you observed that caused someone else misery.

7. Now with all that you understand, how can you work together to correct this problem of privatizing prisons and stop them from profiting from exploiting inmates and their families?

Welcome Home 42

Can I Trust You?

You may not have said that lately, but you thought it. You thought it about another person, a family member, a cop, or your PO.

Can I trust you?

Besides having the most carefully pronounced name in academics, Francis Fukuyama weighed in on this question in a 1995 book called *Trust: The Social Virtues and the Creation of Prosperity.* I think of Fukuyama's book a lot because he has a whole chapter on blacks and asians, looking at how trust supports community economic development. Short version, he says that blacks don't trust one another much, mainly because of the history of slavery and discrimination in America. He cites how they have to be admonished to buy from one another. That's why it was big news when Slim Thug, Paul Wall, Willie D, and Trae The Truth led Houston rap artists to open accounts at Unity National Bank, the only black-owned bank in Texas.

Can I trust you?

That's what we have in the back of our minds when we come home from a bid and somebody wants to help because not everyone who wants to help is someone I can trust. Some people are in it for themselves, whether they want something from you in return or whether they're just doing something good to feel good about themselves. Then they get played, and the game is on.

Can I trust you?

Having someone you trust in your life is critical in successful reentries, such as someone who has your best interest at heart. It's not necessarily someone you trusted before the bid. Look where that got you. And repeating the same patterns will have the same result. You need someone who supports you in making the positive changes necessary to be productive.

That's why Fukuyama (say it slowly) ties it to community development. When we build relationships of trust, we can work together, support one another, even bank together. That's in that chapter on blacks and asians, too, because that's how asians buy up all the stores, through banking together and sharing resources.

Can I trust you?

That's not just a personal question now. It's a social question, too. Trust in law enforcement is at an all-time low. I can't even trust a cop when my hands are up, whether I'm a young boy on the street in Ferguson, a black man being stopped for a traffic violation, or a behavioral therapist rescuing an autistic client from playing in the street. In his book *Don't Shoot: One Man, A Street Fellowship and the End of Violence in Inner-City America,* David Kennedy talks about his 20 years of working with police departments, gangs, and poor neighborhoods. He's clear that none of those three trusts one another. Even the good people in all three operate out of fear, and fear grows where there is no trust.

Can I trust you?

That question framed the Facebook posting of Baton Rouge police officer Montrell Jackson. He expressed the insecurity several days before he was killed when he wrote: "I've experienced so much in my short life, and the past three days have tested me to the core. I swear to God I love this city, but I wonder if this city loves me. In uniform, I get nasty, hateful looks, and out of uniform, some consider me a threat."

Could Officer Jackson trust you? Could Montrell Jackson out of uniform trust you? Was Officer Jackson trusted? Was Montrell Jackson trusted when he was out of uniform? In the end, neither of Montrell Jackson's two sides had enough trust to save his life. But he wanted that trust, and he wanted to offer it to others:

"Please don't let hate infect your heart. This city MUST and WILL get better. I'm working in these streets, so any protesters, officers, friends, family, or whoever, if you see me and need a hug or want to say a prayer, I got you."

Can I trust you?

Questions for Reflection:

1. The author repeatedly says, "Can I trust you?" What does it mean to you?

2. What significance does the phrase have when you think about your relationships with your family, friends, community, and local police, among others?

3. The author states that black people have had trust issues that date back to slavery. My mother used to say, "We black folk are like crabs in a barrel. Once we are in there, you never have to worry. We will not help each other out! We will pull each other down." What have you found faithful to be in your life concerning our relationships with one another?

4. The author cites examples of asians working together to get ahead. In studying the asian culture, they are protective of one another as a family and a society. What is needed for us, as black people, to be more trusting of one another?

5. What skills or talents can you bring to your community to help facilitate trust among the community members?

6. Why is the old adage so important even now in our society and our continuing struggle for equality and liberty for all that says, "United we stand, divided we fall.?

7. I was never so proud to be an American as I was this past summer when blacks, asians, whites, hispanics, and people of all colors peacefully protested together to say, "Black lives matter!" What are you willing to do to demonstrate your trustworthiness and that you can trust?

I Don't Get Mad. I Get Even.

"Payback's a b!+&#!"

"Revenge is sweet."

I know you have heard, probably said, one or both of the above. Revenge feels good. Retaliation rocks! It's an adrenaline rush that releases the frustration of being threatened, attacked, or hurt, whether physically or mentally. It feels good—for the moment. Then the pain comes back, bringing with it a side order of "head-on-a-swivel" because now that you got yours, somebody is coming after you. That's how it works.

Somebody once said, "When you dig someone else's grave, make sure you dig two because one is for you." Revenge only feels good for a little while, but it doesn't change anything.

When I was locked up, a guy on our block made his own set of weights, using uniform tops filled with water and broomsticks. He lifted vigorously every day. The COs would confiscate his homemade weights, and he'd make another set and lift. He had one goal in mind: "I'm gonna [mess] up my brother-in-law for being the snitch that got me in here!"

One day, dude came back to the unit from his work-release job at McDonald's. He was beaming. "My kids came by the shop today, and I got to give them some free hamburgers. I miss them." One of the other guys on the block said, "Yo, you really gonna miss them if you [mess] up your brother-in-law when you get home."

Yeah, taking care of his brother-in-law would be sweet until he'd eventually get picked up and do serious time for that and miss out even more of his kids in a far-off state facility instead of the county jail. "I ain't even think about that," said dude. I wonder what he chose.

We live in a culture of revenge. Don't think for a minute that when candidates call for law and order, they ain't saying, "I want revenge on folk who break the law." When a politician says we have to "bring them to justice," he ain't doin' nothin' but singin' James Brown lyrics: "Get ready you mother', for the big Payback!" Much of the current political talk is about revenge: revenge on immigrants, revenge on Muslims, revenge on black people, revenge on Obama. But the politicians forget that the sweetness is short-lived, and pain will return with that same "head-swivel" side, only now it's supersized.

There's a program out there called CureViolence. It has a simple philosophy: Violence is an epidemic spread by revenge. If you peacefully settle the first beef, it won't escalate into 20 more. It works, but powerful people don't like to support it because it saves too many black and brown lives that would otherwise get chewed and churned and keeps too many of us out of prison because it deescalates violence.

So there are haters on TV every day now trying to get elected. The Republicans held a whole day at their convention in 2016 to "Make America Safe (From You) Again." They lift revenge to a cultural art form. Who will break the cycle?

We need you on the front line. We need you home to be part of the movement that rebuilds our communities, families, and neighborhoods. We need you mentally healthy and to stay alert in the struggle. We need you to show the next generation that there are alternatives to violence and payback. And we need you to vote or mobilize the vote to stop the coronation of revenge as national policy. Is losing all that worth a short moment of sweet revenge?

Questions for Reflection:

1. Are you holding a grudge and seeking revenge, or have you decided to leave the vengeance to a higher power? My mother continually reminded me growing up, "You invariably will reap what you sow; it may not happen today or tomorrow, but, oh, it will come back and bite you in the behind."

2. Why do you suppose the author wrote this piece on revenge and retaliation?

3. How are you wasting your time, energy, and possibly your life on making someone pay for what you believe they have done to you?

4. How can you alter your thought process? What are some of the examples provided by the author in this reflection entry?

5. What are some things you can commit to that would better use your time, energy, and skills?

6. Who do you need to support and help rather than returning to prison to make a point?

7. Is there a purpose that you are ready to commit to that will benefit not only you but possibly your family and community?

The Complaints Started Late Wednesday Night and Ran Over Into Thursday Morning

Anger and frustration boiled hot on the streets of Washington, DC, in January 2016. The target? The snow of over 17 inches and the region's snow removal agencies. The snow came and made travel frustrating and maddening. The region was unprepared for the snow or the traffic. The wailing increased over the weekend when more snow dumped its fury on the entire East Coast, setting records, blocking traffic, canceling events, and making life miserable for thousands upon thousands. But somewhere in the blizzard of snow and cursing was hidden a voice of gratitude.

That's right, gratitude. Because some of us remember what a snowstorm, or any storm, meant for us while locked up or locked down. A storm of that magnitude meant lockdown in your cell while corrections staff fretted over a power outage. Forget being cooped up in your house for two days. Try being crowded in a two-man cell with three residents for two days, one of you sleeping by the toilet, and no Febreeze, yo, courtesy flush notwithstanding.

Gratitude because thousands of family members were denied the possibility of a prison visit on a snowy weekend. Kids couldn't see their mamas or daddies, mothers could not visit their sons or daughters, siblings stayed home, and grandparents wailed over lost time and money invested in a potential visit. A friend of mine who did federal time mentioned how the snow reminded her of the loneliness of her bid; it highlighted what it means to be cut off from friends and family. Yes, gratitude.

I could go outside, breathe cold fresh air, and shovel when the blizzard stopped. I got to watch children playing. I saw young black men—stereotyped as lazy do-nothings—turn into entrepreneurs with shovels. And I watched icicles form from trees, not watchtowers. Just Gratitude.

Whenever trouble comes, perspective is in order. You can look at it as a problem that overwhelms you or as a challenge to be accepted. Whether you are struggling to find a job or involved in the struggle to change criminal justice laws that make it hard to find jobs, perspective can be the difference between success and repeated failure. Gratitude starts with being thankful for how far we have come and the opportunities we have to make it work this time. Even working on gratitude for little things such as running water, a warm shower, and a room bigger than a cell can build the muscles of faith that support your best efforts at being productive.

Or you can be like the agencies in DC, unprepared for a small storm, turning a little challenge into a big mess. And the cursing, anger, and frustration will be heard again.

Questions for Reflection:
1. As you think back on your bid, what are you grateful for as a returning citizen when it comes to living through snowstorms?

2. Why do you suppose the author says, "Whenever trouble comes, perspective is in order."? How does perspective help to give you clarity to the circumstance you are dealing with?

3. To you, what is the difference between looking at problems as something that overwhelms you or as a challenge to be accepted? Do you see the positivity of this thought by the author? If not, what is the belief or obstacle preventing you from seeing the meaning?

4. Are you a thought-driven person or an emotion-, feeling-, or reactive-driven person? Do you see any dangers in being an emotion or reactive-driven person? Why or why not?

5. Think about what the author is saying when he states, "Whether you are struggling to find a job, or involved in the struggle to change criminal justice laws that make it hard to find jobs, perspective can be the difference between success and repeated failure." What is this statement saying to you based on your understanding of the words "feelings" vs. "thinking"?

6. Are you ready to begin the process of being grateful? Realizing that the author defines *gratitude* as being in the state of "being thankful for how far you and I have come, and the opportunities we have to make it work this time.? Why or why not?

7. Take time to get quiet thinking about those things that need to be on your gratitude list and why they are beneficial to you. How can you move forward to help someone else to be grateful?

Welcome Home 45

You Are Valuable! You Have Self-Worth

He was charged with five counts of attempted murder of a police officer. Law enforcement and government officials suspect him of planting bombs in New York and New Jersey, one of which injured more than two dozen people. The cops he tried to kill shot him in the leg. He's alive and in the hospital.

Meanwhile, Sondra Bland's traffic offense, Eric Garner's loose cigarette's, Michael Brown's hands up, Tamir Brown's toy gun, Philando Castile's wallet, Terrence Crutcher's stalled truck, Daunte Wright's air freshener, George Floyd's money, Breonna Taylor's address, and Walter Scott's child support got them killed by police. What's the difference?

In Elizabeth, New Jersey, the police didn't kill Ahmad Rahami in 2016 because he was valuable. More specifically, he had valuable intelligence. Was he part of a terrorist cell? Who were his accomplices? He had traveled to Pakistan within the last year. Who did he meet? Is he connected to ISIS or some other crucial terrorist organization? He had intel. He was valuable. He wasn't killed or subjected to lethal force. He was valuable.

Damn it, all of those people who died at the hands of the police were valuable. Their value stemmed from their being made by the Creator, who values all life. The system may not recognized it, but they had value. They still have value as we reflect on their memory to energize communities and a nation to stop the unjust killings and devaluation of human life.

You have value. And it comes from your Creator. It doesn't matter how many bids you have done, how long your jacket is, how much time you have before you get off paper. (I have 166 more days before I get off paper and out of the system for the first time in ten years.) But also, you have value because you have valuable intelligence. There are things you know that the world needs, your community needs, your family needs. You have valuable intel.

Only you have the intel that a father or a mother can give the children they brought into the world. Only you have the intel that present, future, and grandchildren need to know the joy of sitting in Mom's lap or on Pop Pop's knee. Only you have the intel to share your story with young people who need to know how to avoid the mistakes you made. Only you have the intel to take your story and pool it with other stories, and become part of a movement that commands respect from the community, government, and law enforcement.

Is it any wonder some of us can't vote? Those of us who have made the changes and embraced our valuable intel could provide a significant voting bloc against the forces that don't value what we know and do not value or respect our lives. That's one reason you should vote this November if you can and motivate others to vote if you can't. Valuable intel says that you are a person of worth and dignity "endowed by the Creator with certain inalienable rights," even if the author of those words didn't believe them himself.

But it starts with believing it yourself. I have a young relative who has struggled with substances, mental illness, and the system. He's currently on paper in the same county as I was. He confided in me his self-doubts a few days ago, citing the system's

failure to take him seriously, despite his intelligence, writing ability, and a degree from a credible college. I tried to talk with him
about our inherent self-worth and not let the system's devaluation define him. Then I saw what happened in Elizabeth, New
Jersey. I hope he reads this column. He has valuable intel.

Questions for Reflection:

1. The author said you are valuable because the divine Creator made you. Do you believe this? Why or why not? Do you
believe in yourself? If not, what are some of your limiting
beliefs about yourself? List some of your valuable traits.

2. What does healthy self-esteem mean to you? What do you
envision healthy self-esteem to be? Spend quiet time ponder-
ing when you feel self-sufficient and able. Train yourself to
spend time to do these positive self-sufficient or autonomous
things.

3. Is your self-esteem a product of positive self-talk (or the
opposite)?

4. Do you doubt your professional or personal competence?

5. How can you transform painful experiences or events from the past into positive lessons?

6. Thinking about what you are good at, how can you help others with your unique skills, talents, and qualities?

7. How often do you fall victim to other people's opinions? List activities you can practice to stop your overvaluation of others' opinions and avoid negative self-talk. List your core values and beliefs.

We Need You

I know you have enough personal drama, but we need you.

Family issues, job worries, trying to make the adjustment home, but we need you.

PO drama, compliance crap, but we need you.

We interrupt this personal broadcast of life drama to repeat it: "We need you!"

We need your voice. We need your presence because the system is broken. We, people under some form of supervision by a broken criminal justice system, know what needs to be fixed because, as Glenn Martin, founder of JustLeadershipUSA, regularly says, "Those who are closest to the problem are closest to the solution."

I tried to buy a local paper at the train station one day, but they didn't have it. So I purchased *USA Today*. The front page was filled with stories that say, "We need you!"

First, there is a story about the high number of police chiefs resigning in the flood of allegations of police misconduct, killings of unarmed black men and women, and police corruption. Relationships between law enforcement and the community show little trust on either side, and somebody has to get busy putting this stuff back together. Jeffrey Brown, a Boston-based minister, has been traveling North America to help bridge the gap between police and their communities. Nobody is saying we don't need cops; but through his Operation RECAP, Brown says that we need to get it right concerning their role in our neighborhoods. Rev. Brown needs you!

Then, there is a story about the acquittal of one of the Baltimore police officers in the death of Freddie Gray, who died in police custody. Black Lives Matter protesters hold their signs on the front page picture while reactionary voices counter with Blue Lives Matter legislation making assaulting a cop a hate crime.

With each annual election, progress is being made to secure you the vote. In Pennsylvania, you can vote, even if you have a felony conviction. You can vote from jail if you are there on a misdemeanor. I followed a city jail warden around the block once, passing out absentee ballots to misdemeanor residents. She cried out, "Y'all need to vote. The judges are up for election this year, and y'all know them better than we do!" The ballot box needs you!

Suppose you live in a state that doesn't let you vote. In that case, there are people like Desmond Meade, director of Faith in Florida, who is among several people who agitated for the right to vote, even if you have a felony conviction, and continues to fight to keep Florida's Proposition 4 from destruction. He should know. He has been homeless, strung out, and locked up. But by God's grace, he got clean and sober, came home, finished school, got his law degree (even though he is barred from practicing in Florida), and now leads the statewide charge to restore and retain voting rights to people like himself. Desmond Meade and people like him need you.

Finally, the paper has a story on the Supreme Court's 7-1 decision to release a death row inmate in Georgia. His prosecutor stacked the deck on his jury by deliberately excluding black people. Even his defense attorney—since disbarred—wouldn't call a witness who could place him in another state at the time of the murder. (I won't tell you which Justice voted against the release, but his name rhymes with No Mas.)

JustLeadershipUSA is mounting a national movement of formerly incarcerated people to take leadership in reducing mass incarceration. They work to improve justice in a nation that produces such wrongful convictions that involve every level of the criminal justice system. Their work includes bringing reforms from policing to parole, from the courtroom to the cell block. JustLeadership USA needs you.

I don't know what your drama is today. But I know that there is somebody in your area who is taking on the very powers that have taken your mistakes and made them worse. People like Jondhi Harrell of The Center for Returning Citizens in Philadelphia and Jerry Blassingame of Soteria CDC in South Carolina labor tirelessly on our behalf despite their drama since coming home.

Your drama may seem overwhelming, but it can help press the pause button, look around at what needs to be changed, and hook up with change agents in your community. You are needed to be part of the larger solution. It will help you get out of yourself by working for the bigger change that will benefit you and others.

We need you.

Questions for Reflection:

1. After reading "We Need You," think seriously, considering where you fit in working to right wrongs in the criminal justice system and the community.

2. What are your most essential skills, and how can you use them to help create an equitable criminal justice system?

3. What qualities do you admire in at least two of the people mentioned in this reading? Why do their mentioned traits motivate you?

4. Given your qualities and traits, how can you assist in the struggle to improve the criminal justice system?

5. In the state or commonwealth in which you live, what is the condition of relations between the police and your communities?

6. Do you know the political climate and how it impacts your state, county, and local justice system? If you don't, how will you attempt to found out?

7. Are you ready to get serious and find ways to help, be it part-time, full-time, or in your volunteer time? If yes, list where you will start in your journal and then get started. If not, what is holding you back and why?

Dead Man Walking

Dead Man Walking. In prison, it's an actual call. You can hear the chains and the boots. In life, it's a feeling of despair. You can hear the negative voices and feelings. We often felt that despair in jail, and sometimes it comes back to haunt us when we get home.

Not Nikki.

Nikki Roberts has hope today, but it didn't come easy. Nikki has a hope she can live, breathe, and preach. When you talk to her, it becomes apparent that her hope is neither wishful thinking nor blind optimism. She has hope today, which, interestingly, came as a gift and with a price.

Nikki received hope in a place usually reserved for pain and despair. She received it from someone society had already written off as dead. "Dead man walking" became "Dead woman testifying" as she sat in the LockDown unit in the Georgia women's prison after multiple suicide attempts. "I was put in solitary," she says, "upset that I was still alive." She was "crying out in disgust" at the failed attempts at suicide. Voices echoed in her memory of others in the facility who had encouraged her to pack it in, but a live voice breathed through the air vent and into her cell.

"You do not belong to this system," said the voice in one of several "hope-laden messages." "You do not belong to your mistakes; you belong to God." For three weeks, the voice offered encouragement through the ventilation system. The voice had no face—women on lockdown rarely saw each other—but it had a name: Kelly. Kelly Gissendaner, a name infamous in Georgia criminal culture, the only woman on that state's death row, sentenced to death for the murder of her husband, was speaking life to Nikki.

Kelly told Nikki how her life had been changed by studying theology. It was her way of making sense of her life, life choices, and current situation. Kelly was on a quest for meaning, one to which we all are called but often fail to answer. Being in prison was not enough to make her think about her life and choices. But the volunteers from Emory University's Candler School of Theology who came to the prison had given Kelly a chance to think about what her life meant and to conclude that despite her past, her life was worth something. She had to believe that, otherwise, she wouldn't have been able to tell Nikki that *her* life mattered.

For a while, Kelly was allowed to go to the theology class. Chained and surrounded by the CERT Team (if you don't know that, you ain't been to jail or prison). She was marched to class with the traditional Dead Man Walking call that signaled the other prisoners to turn their backs to her trek to the classroom. But that "dead man" became a live woman in theology class. When the warden revoked Kelly's privilege of attending class, the volunteers pursued and won the ability to go on her block and teach her through the gate.

Kelly's hope rushed through the air vent to Nikki, who decided to study theology and meet these hope-filled volunteers. No small thing for Nikki, who the prison case manager had told was ineligible for pursuing answers to a blank treatment assessment because "you got too much time left to see me. Get out my line!"

Kelly's voice combated Nikki's negative self-talk and convinced her to seek an interview into the program. Once accepted, she found encouragement from the volunteers and the other inmates in the program. "I needed to be engaged with others on the journey," she said. "I was 'humanized,' made eye contact, got called by my name" in the classroom.

Nikki had come from a religious family, but this was different. She was discovering her faith anew, and the ability to ask questions, study, and have discussions about faith made her feel "liberated while still confined."

Nikki's hope today continues in her second year home from prison. She has a future for herself. It's a gift, but it had a price. Kelly Gissandaner was executed on September 30, 2015. "Dead Man Walking" became "Live Angel Rising," as her remorse and repentance could not save her earthly life but guaranteed a heavenly one. And she lives on in Nikki Roberts and so many others that her discovery and hope touched.

Do you ever feel like a Dead Man Walking? Have you been written off, told you would never amount to anything? Nikki Roberts was gifted hope by someone who was as good as dead, as far as society was concerned. Imagine what you can do with your time left here.

Questions for Reflection:

1. Does the phrase *Dead Man Walking* have meaning in your life?

2. Have you felt as if you were locked down or locked out? Write down the feelings that you experienced. What was the cause of you experiencing these feelings?

3. Have you ever attempted or thought about committing suicide? Have you sought help? If not, why not? If yes, who helped you through the experience?

4. How did the person or persons help you? What did they say that made a difference?

5. What are you doing now to stay mentally healthy and able?

6. What are you doing to make your trial or struggle help someone else?

7. What have you gained from learned lessons that will make your struggles and challenges achieve your state of hope?

13th

"Doc, you gotta watch *13th*!"

I heard that a million times after the new Netflix documentary *13th* came out. It's about how the system of mass incarceration evolved from slavery. It takes its name from the thirteenth amendment, which abolishes slavery in the United States, except imprisonment.

"I don't need to see that stuff," I said to myself, actually using a more earthy noun relegating the documentary to fecal waste matter. "I lived it." I don't watch *Bad Boys* or any other cop show. I don't watch reality prison TV; I don't watch *Orange Is the New Black* because my mentor Glenn Martin reminds us that "Black is the new orange." I marveled at the guys on my block watching the movie *Life* and laughing at prison scenes. I don't need to watch no damn documentary to learn that stuff. I lived it, teach it, and teach in it. I ain't gonna learn nothing.'

Or so I thought.

I showed it to a group of university students one day. I learned a lot.

No, I learned nothing new about the system; how it works; the inhumanity; the beat downs; the lockdowns; the unjust sentencing practices; and the war on drugs, which is a war on people of color who use drugs. That's not anything I learned.

I learned just how uninformed this country is about the reality of how our criminal justice system exploits, oppresses and dehumanizes us all.

The students in the class asked good questions. They were motivated, but their questions reflected a certain sheltering from the realities of prison and jail. I won't call it ignorance (more on that later), but I will say that we have sanitized the system through dumb, pithy phrases such as "If you can't do the time, don't do the crime." Or through demonizing and criminalizing behaviors that require treatment and not punishment so we can "lock 'em up and throw away the key."

The buzz created by *13th* lies in part in just how little many people know about how we got to this point. Many did not realize that the thirteenth amendment makes slavery legal for incarcerated persons. Guys in the Texas prison system know it because if you refuse to work there with little or sometimes no pay, you get put in solitary. Slavery is even part of alternative sentencing when you have to choose between unpaid labor and jail time. People don't see the connection between that and the "convict leasing" they talk about in *13th*.

People know little about what it means to be human. The documentary shows black garbage men in Memphis in 1968, striking, marching with signs, saying, "I Am a Man!" People don't see that this is what incarcerated people are saying. It's what we are saying when we get home with labels such as *ex-con*, *felon*, and *ex-offender* that stigmatize us and keep us from full participation in the job market, housing, and education.

People don't know. Sorry, now it's time for the word. People are just plain ignorant to the connection between today's world and our history. How else can you explain the Trump phenomenon? The documentary closes with audio of Trump calling for "the good old days," when demonstrators got "punched in the mouth and carried off on a stretcher." While playing Trump's audio, the documentary shows Civil Rights demonstrators being punched, hosed, attacked by dogs, and carried off on stretchers. That's the good old days? Ignorant.

By the way, if you can vote and don't, you're ignorant, too. Even if you don't like who is running for president, there are Senate, House, state, county, and local elections that determine who will make the next set of laws about criminalization and sentencing, supervise the prison and jails, oversee probation and parole, allocate money for educational institutions and correctional facilities.

That ain't a federal affair; it's your city council, state reps, sheriffs, district attorneys, and people like that. And if you can vote and don't, you're ignorant. I'll take it a step further. If you can't vote, find five people who can, and make sure they vote. You, too, can combat ignorance in the people around you. Hell, show them *13th* if you have to. I'd hate to see ignorance win on Election Day.

Questions for Reflection:

1. Have you seen Netflix's movie *13th*? If you have, what are your thoughts about it?

2. What does the author want you to understand from this entry?

3. Why is it so vital for people of color and marginalized people not to be ignorant of today's issues and matters?

4. Why is it essential to understand how racism, bigotry, and slavery of yesteryears are attempting to be reinstituted or reenacted today by some?

5. Do you know what "convict leasing" is? What can you do to help change such policies on the local, county, and state levels?

6. If you don't know what convict leasing is, research it and then decide what you can do to change this loophole.

7.There is a big difference between ignorance and being reckless and unwise. For instance, not knowing something is ignorance, but not doing something once you know what is going on is ridiculous. People who could have voted but did not vote in the 2016 election were irresponsible. What are your thoughts on the matter? How will your thoughts encourage you to act concerning future elections?

Welcome Home 49

Remembering Can Be a Good Thing!

I know what it's like to be separated from family on Christmas Day. I know what it's like to have a Christmas dinner featuring roast beef tips from the meatpacking plant that employs work-release guys. I don't ever want to experience that again.

We talked elsewhere in this book about keeping straight for the holidays. It always applies. But for some of us, there will be the pain of separation. Some will wake up Christmas morning on a cold mattress, wondering if anyone remembers they are there.

Maybe someone you know needs a visit or a card to let them know they are not forgotten. If you don't have a visitor's clearance to a correctional facility, you may know a family member of that person left behind. There may be a grieving mother, an anxious spouse, a wondering child. Drop by, give them a call; they feel the pain of separation, too. It can break some of the tension and ease some of the loneliness, or it may be you feel that pain. Know that someone is praying for you.

But not just for them, for you too. One of the things they teach in the rooms of recovery is that a good way to stop your pity party is to get out of yourself and do something for someone else. I'd tell you to shovel somebody's snow, but it looks like we are having a warm Christmas in most of the country. But sweep a walk, give someone a ride, buy a small unexpected gift, expecting nothing in return. There is someone impacted by incarceration whose day you can brighten today. Writing this to you has helped my day already, and the holiday isn't over yet. I need to bring a few more smiles into the world and dry a few more tears. Join me.

Questions for Reflection:

1. The author states that one of the things they teach in the rooms of recovery is that a good way to stop your pity party is to get out of yourself and do something for someone else. How does helping others call you out of your self-pity and despair?

2. Have you experienced similar feelings or actual pain during the holidays like the author? If so, write down in your journal what you felt and what you did to cope.

3. Did someone extend advice or tips to you on how to make it through the holidays? If so, what were some of the more positive ones that you can draw on or pass on to others?

4. Make a list of things you can do for others. What is some small gesture of kindness that you can start doing for others? Why this particular gesture or gift?

5. Have you known someone who was or is incarcerated or a person's loved one who was or is suffering from loneliness? What positive thing did you do for them that lightened his or her load?

6. How did that positive act of kindness that you did impact you? Explore this for a moment.

7. Did you have a sense of satisfaction from this act of kindness? Write down your feelings in your journal.

You Already Know the Deal

After dealing with the school system, you know the deal. After struggling with the economic system, you know the deal. The way you were treated through the criminal justice system, from arrest to detention, court, to your bid, and then home, tells me you already know the deal.

The emergence of divisive politics didn't change America; it revealed America. We knew how this country felt about us, despite the efforts of a merciful few and a few politicians looking to save money for taxpayers while appearing to care about us. We knew, and now the world knows.

So since you knew, you are not surprised. And since you're not surprised, first of all, don't act like you didn't know. You can protest, but leave the violent confrontation to someone else. You know better, so do better. And it's not an "I told you so" moment, because all that does is get people on the defensive, trying to prove their progressive credentials.

No, it's time to ask questions: "Now that this stuff is out in the open, from the Big House to the farmhouse to the White House, how will we live?" "How will I make this country better for my children and grandchildren?" "How can I make America great for the first time?"

Here's my list:

(1) I'm praying not so much because I am religious (I am), but because I need to remind myself that something greater than the madness has unfolded. Looking at the enlarged picture of the moon; taking time to look at the sky and the trees; and listening to birds reminds me that there is something greater than any political party. I never played basketball when we had yard on my block (I stink at it anyway). I found the places where the grass grew through the asphalt and cement. Each day, I grabbed a blade of grass to remind me that the world was bigger than my block and that there is a force greater than COs playing god. And stopping to breathe in the air, as well as picking up a few blades of grass today, reminds me that there is still something greater, and the new administration does not have the last word on my humanity.

(2) I'm checking up on my friends still on paper, still struggling with their reentry and those ridiculous sanctions that make it harder to find work, housing, education, citizenship, and any other foolishness they deal with to remind them of their status as an "ex-offender." I won't call them an "ex- anything"; I'll call them by name and help them know their humanity. I won't look at them as animals, thugs, felons, or anything other than the men or women God created them to be. I'll talk with them, commiserate with them, cry, or anything else with them that helps them adjust and cope, not to the reality of the "new America," but the revelation of what we were like all along.

(3) I'm ramping up my work to dismantle mass incarceration and replace it with more humane and just forms of dealing with human behavior. That includes investing time as a volunteer in schools, prisons, jails, and the barbershop. That includes joining protesting voices outside the White House and inside the classroom. That includes writing to anyone who will read that the world hasn't ended, and the struggle continues. I'm renewing

my membership in JustLeadership USA, the nation's leading organization of formerly incarcerated persons, in the belief of the words of founder Glenn Martin: "Those who are closest to the problem are closest to the solution." I'm having students read Nicole Gonzalez Van Cleve's *Crook County* so they can see firsthand what it's like to move through the front end of the court system with degreed professionals in coats, ties, dresses, and robes calling you a "mope" or a "monster." I'm giving and telling my friends to give to organizations such as Equal Justice Initiative, ScholarChips, LiveFree, and other groups leading the charge against unjust sentencing, unfair treatment, and alternatives to incarceration.

(4) I'm going to check myself. I'm going to see where I have contributed to a nation that allows foolishness to flourish. I'm going to go back over my list of those who were hurt by my incarceration, indeed, my behavior that led to incarceration. For it is my responsibility to make sure I've made things right with them. No sense going after liars and cheats in government if I'm one myself. I gotta clean house in my personal administration before I go after a political administration. I'm not perfect, but I can be a lot better. And this country can, too. I'm working on it.

Questions for Reflection:

1. The author challenged himself in this piece: "Now that this stuff is out in the open, from the Big House to the farmhouse to the White House, how will we live?" What is your response to his challenge? Write your answer in your journal, and be completely honest with yourself.

2. The author posed a second salient question: "How will I make this country better for my children and grandchildren?"

What is your comeback to his query? Meditate over your answer, and be candid and committed to doing something.

3. Since the previous White House occupant tarnished the word *great*, how would you make America the best it can be?

4. From the author's list of things he is doing under (1) spiritually and in thanksgiving or gratitude to your Creator, which ones will you commit to doing and why?

5. Under (2), the author's list of things to help and encourage others, which of his listed items will you work on and why? List others that you think of that he did not mention.

6. Under (3), the author lists his advocacy work efforts. Do you have aspirations of getting involved? If so, why and how and with which organizations?

7. Under (4), the author discusses how he will self-evaluate and change his behavior, bridle his tongue, and revert negative self-talk into positive talk. What methods of self-evaluation and behavior reversal will you work on to make you a more positive, empathetic, and patient person?

It Started With the Beef Tips

That's right, beef tips.

I was at my mother's apartment in the senior citizen's complex, getting ready to head down to dinner. She asked me to look at the menu, and there it was: beef tips. Something clicked in my mind, reading that weekly menu posted on the wall.

When we sat down to eat, the server brought the meal. Beef tips! Damn! I remember now! The last time I ate beef tips was December 25, 2010, in jail!

The menu posted on the wall should have been a reminder. I felt bad, but I couldn't put my finger on why. But when the beef tips came, I remembered. It was a flashback, another flashback to being in jail. The menu on the wall and the damn beef tips. They smelled like jail!

I know the day we got the beef tips because it was Christmas. We had awakened to see the walls and wire. The TV reminded us what day it was, as if we didn't know. We were separated from family and friends. We had kids and grandkids opening presents, taking pictures, having dinner—all without us. So to make us feel "special" on Christmas, the jail had deviated from its usual diet of processed mystery meat to give us beef tips. (Even that delicacy was courtesy of the meat processing plant that employed the work-release guys for pennies an hour).

Flashbacks are a bit of a problem, and we have all had them. Sometimes it's a sound or a sight that stimulates. Sometimes it's a dream I have at least once a week, like the one last week where I was sentenced to a conspiracy charge connected to 9/11. But your mind is scarred. The deprivation of liberty, the shouting and confrontations, the COs acting out their need for supremacy masking as security—it all comes back.

You try to take steps to distance yourself. For one thing, I never eat Ramen noodles now; and to my friend who gave me a pack as a gag gift a few years back, just be glad I'm a Christian, because that stuff wasn't funny. I don't shop in certain stores and companies because they were part of the money-making schemes complicit in our incarceration.

When I go through the security checkpoints at the airport, I thank God that at least I didn't have to drop, squat, and cough. When I took my pee test—sorry, "urinalysis"—to get clearance to teach a class at a local jail, I was glad that at least nobody was looking over my shoulder. (By the way, I told the CO who apologized to me for having to watch me pee, uh, urinate in jail that I felt sorry for him, having a job where you have to watch dozens of grown men pee.) There are just so many reminders.

The only good thing about the memories is that they "keep it green" not just to remind me of my new purpose in life, but also to stay awake and help others with their adjustment back home. They remind me to stay awake and go back to the facility tonight to talk to the brothers about being spiritually and emotionally healthy. They remind me to stay awake and work to dismantle this corrupt criminal justice system and seek to implement more just means of dealing with our brothers and sisters. They remind me to stay awake and turn nightmares into dreams and visions.

And it started with beef tips.

Questions for Reflections:

1. The remembrance of beef tips on Christmas Day while incarcerated opened the floodgate of hurtful, bitter, and painful memories for the author. What memories cause you to remember cruel, harsh, and raw treatment during your bid?

2. In order not to relive these punitive and inhumane experiences, the author states he avoids certain things. What practice have you taken to prevent similar memories? List them in your journal, so you identify your triggers.

3. The author stated that he gives thanks to God for even the small improvements in his treatment outside of prison, such as walking in airports. What small and big improvements do you thank God for that have occurred in your treatment?

4. Also, the author talked about how he shared his lessons learned with the other brothers incarcerated with him. Do you recall what you shared with others to make their incarceration smoother or more bearable?

5. Now that you are home, what are you sharing to help reentering citizens improve their emotional and spiritual health?

6. Have you thought about how you will become involved in assisting reentering citizens to adjust to being home?

7. How are you planning to change your nightmares into dreams for your future and the future of your children, grand-children, and other loved ones?

Holiday Presence

I was sitting in my recovery support group one weekend while we discussed ways of staying clean and sober over the holidays. It got me thinking about things we have to be careful about during the holidays as people coming home from prison.
I asked a number of people I know who have successfully met the challenge. Everyone agreed that we have to avoid alcohol and drugs. I laughed about that one because I try to stay away from those on any day ending in *y*.

Making sure we are not around people who are carrying or still involved in illegal activities came up more than once. For many of us, that's a condition of parole or probation, and one-third of state prison admissions are for violations.

One person talked about the emotional pressure with succeeding during the holiday, one must lavish gifts on family at a time when he or she can't possibly afford to purchase such gifts. Churches and friends could show love and assist that individual in seeing the value of first bringing a present, not necessarily giving a present. If able to assist with getting gifts, supportive people should first focus on the joy of belonging home. Presence beats presents.

On a positive note, we can reflect on the true meaning of the season, whether Christmas, New Year's, Kwanzaa, a time to reconnect with family and friends committed to supporting us in making changes necessary for positive reintegration into the community.

One pastor, who leads a congregation in Philadelphia made up primarily of formerly incarcerated persons and their families offered this: "I find that most who have been incarcerated for long periods are overwhelmed by the world they encounter. It is often very different from what they envisioned, and even though they have spent much time planning and getting ready for release, they find that the plans they made will not work in a world they know very little about. Much of the work we do at LIFE Ministry at Living Gospel is emotional support and self-esteem building during the first month or so after release for those who have been away from the community for long periods."

She says that it is crucial for those who want to help to understand that they do not have to know how to do it all. "Knowing where to send folks to get the resources and support they need is also extremely important. In our zeal to be helpful, we often do the exact opposite by giving folks information that is incorrect or out of date; being aware of the resources in your community can often be the best addition to your toolbox."

There is support for us in this season, but we also have to take responsibility for our own decisions. Be well, and be careful this holiday season. I've had prison roast beef on Christmas. I'll take turkey at home this year.

Questions for Reflections:
1. The author makes an excellent point when he wrote, "Everyone agreed that we have to avoid alcohol and drugs. I laughed about that one because I try to stay away from those on any day ending in *y*." How would you define the differing definitions between *trying* and *training*? *Trying* means essentially that one is attempting to do something while exercising or determinedly drilling oneself in doing something is

training. How does training your mind and desires to avoid temptation or the pull of drugs and alcohol change your will when thinking about any and every day ending in *y*?

2. Besides understanding it is a violation of law to go around people who are holding, why should it be imperative to you not to be around people who are holding or involved in illegal activity?

3. Why is it imperative to be on your guard during the holidays, leading up to the holiday season, and after the holiday season?

4. The author provides positive resources to obtaining gifts for loved ones during the holidays. When you are most lacking in funds to provide for gifts, how ready are you to put aside your selfish pride to seek assistance?

5. Realizing that you are ready to ask for help, which resources provided by the author are you willing to proactively pursue to assist you in fulfilling holiday needs for the loved ones in your life?

6. Now that you are training to be preemptive in avoiding drugs and alcohol, what are you most thankful for this holiday season?

7. Since you are actively training to be preemptive in avoiding drugs and alcohol, how do you feel? Are you getting plenty of rest, exercise, and taking time to spend quality time understanding yourself?

Changin' Your Game Plan

How to use Incarceration as a stepping stone to SUCCESS

$30,619.85
a year ($83.89 per day)
is the average cost to keep your loved one locked up physically

$29.99
is the cost
to free him or her mentally

randykearse.co/holidayspecial

CPSIA information can be obtained
at www.ICGtesting.com
Printed in the USA
JSHW040944220922
30842JS00003B/4